CHRISTIANS IN THE PUBLIC SQUARE

Christians
IN THE
Public Square

Faith That Transforms Politics

ELLEN OTT MARSHALL

Abingdon Press
Nashville

CHRISTIANS IN THE PUBLIC SQUARE
FAITH THAT TRANSFORMS POLITICS

Copyright © 2008 by Abingdon Press

This book is printed on acid-free paper.

Library of Congress Cataloging-in-Publication Data

Marshall, Ellen Ott, 1970-
  Christians in the public square : faith that transforms politics / Ellen Ott Marshall.
    p. cm.
  ISBN 978-0-687-64698-2 (binding: pbk. : alk. paper)
  1. Christianity and politics—United States. I. Title.
  BR516.M275 2008
  261.7—dc22

2008022333

08 09 10 11 12 13 14 15 16 17—10 9 8 7 6 5 4 3 2 1
MANUFACTURED IN THE UNITED STATES OF AMERICA

For my parents, Karen and Phil

Contents

Acknowledgments

This book began as a lecture delivered at the Claremont School of Theology in the fall of 2004. My first debt of gratitude, therefore, goes to faculty colleagues who both affirmed the lecture and challenged me to develop it further. I am particularly grateful to Andy Dreitcer for his ongoing interest in this project and to Rich Amesbury, Debbie Roberts, and Frank Rogers for their helpful comments on the manuscript. I value the input and friendship of these four individuals tremendously. I am also fortunate to have truly thoughtful students whose engagement with questions of faith and politics has informed my understanding. I am especially grateful to Katie Schubert for her research assistance and to Katy Scrogin for her careful proofreading and indexing. I also appreciate the support and freedom that Bob Ratcliff extended to me.

I continue to receive immeasurable support from my family and friends. I would be unable to pursue my vocation without their love and the many forms of care they provide. Tommy and Katherine add laughter and levity to my life, and they keep me connected to aspects of the world (like country music and princesses, respectively) that I would not follow on my own. In relationship to this book, I am especially grateful to my mom, Karen, who put her life on hold to be with us when the threat of preterm labor relegated me to bed rest and the arrival of our twins, Zoe and Steve, happily complicated our lives. During this time, Mom not only took care of all aspects of our home life but also enabled me to finish the semester and this manuscript. I am profoundly grateful for her help and friendship, and I am genuinely humbled by the depth of her commitment to the people she loves. There is nothing romantic about my mom's form of commitment. She simply "sticks to it" regardless of the nature of the task and the temperament of the one cared for. Having someone like this to rely on is surely one of life's most precious gifts.

Refusing to Play Politics with Faith

Conflicts and Confrontation

One Monday morning I received an email from a man who had heard me preach some of this book's content the Sunday before. He wrote, "When you started preaching, I thought, 'Here we go again—another liberal who is going to bash my conservative views.' But it wasn't like that at all." This is not a book intended to bash anyone's views. Indeed, it is in large part motivated by the lamentable observation that the expectation of "bashing" is so understandable. I have come to expect bashing whenever I hear a certain tone on the radio or television, whenever a certain position is mentioned in even the most cursory way, and whenever particular names, churches, seminaries, or organizations are referenced authoritatively. And I see similar expectations on the faces of my students every day. When one person begins speaking, those with different theological and political positions ready themselves for assault and rebuttal. In the next moment, as the listeners speak up, the postures become reversed.

We respond to this expectation of bashing by not listening to certain radio stations or watching certain programs, by refusing to read particular publications or listen to particular speakers, by avoiding people who believe "those" things, and by avoiding topics that "get us into trouble." We spend as much time as possible with the programs, people, organizations, and literature that support our own point of view and bash the others. And we do much more than bash other views; we bash the people who hold them. If the only expectation were for disagreement, and if this is what we experienced, then there would be no need for this book. But we expect and experience hatred, personal insult, and offense to our deepest convictions.

On my way to work, I drive two four-year-old girls to preschool. Katherine is my daughter, and Ally is her friend. Every morning, there is some harmony and some kind of disagreement; sometimes the harmony dominates and sometimes the disagreements do. They disagree about whether the clouds are moving on Katherine's side of the car or only on Ally's. They disagree about which song to listen to next or which characters I should include in the story I'm telling. They disagree about whether the song goes "Scooby Scooby Doo" or "Scooby Dooby Doo." Truthfully, there is no end to the subjects on which they can disagree. When I can, I try to help them come to some kind of agreement, but often their disagreements persist and even turn mean. They scold each other or declare that the friendship is over. And so, at least weekly, I find myself saying, "Girls? Girls. Girls! Really, you must find some way to disagree without being mean to each other. It is OK to disagree, but it is not OK to be mean."

Although the subjects of disagreement addressed in this book are significantly more serious, my basic point is the same. We must find some way to disagree without being mean to each other. We must identify ways to work for justice without being consumed by hatred. We must learn how to advocate a position without demonizing the person who thinks differently. And we must find language to express faith's influence on our politics without claiming to have sole or complete knowledge of God's will. In order to accomplish these tasks (or at least move in their direction), I recommend that we practice *agape* in situations of heated conflict, acknowledge and attend to moral ambiguity, and adopt a posture of theological humility.

Playing Politics?

This book assumes that people of faith must bring their religious convictions to bear on political matters. We must do so because our faith is a deeply held part of who we are and therefore cannot be excised. We cannot somehow cut off the "faith portion" and leave it at home or at church as we move out into public spaces. Indeed, the religious tradition that informs us personally informs the way we understand the world and our responsibilities to it. At a minimum, it is dishonest to keep this aspect of our identity and this informing source in stealth mode as we participate in democracy. Refusing to disclose the role of religion in our thinking also excludes faith from the process of critical reflection and engagement in which it must participate.

Those of us in the Christian tradition must bring our faith into the public square for another reason as well. I believe that at the heart of the Christian faith is a social gospel, a call to respond to the needs of the world and those who occupy it. This call has social, political, economic, and ecological implications, and we cannot live out this vocation fully without engaging politics, among other things. This underlying assumption propels me to address a "how" question rather than to debate a "whether" question. The question driving this book is not whether to bring faith into politics, but *how* to do so without playing politics with our faith.

Playing politics with our faith means that we allow the religious tradition that informs us to be used instrumentally in a political process. This is not to suggest that politics is all bad and thus taints religion when they mix. The point is, rather, that there are problematic features of politics that make use of similarly problematic features in religion. This book focuses on three instrumental uses of Christianity in contemporary U.S. politics and recommends three corresponding commitments that, if practiced, can transform politics in some positive ways. These commitments are unconditional love, moral ambiguity, and theological humility.

The Politics of Division

The first problematic feature of politics is that it not only employs disagreement, but also tends to turn those disagreements into walls of division. Disagreement is an unavoidable and even integral part of a political process. This, in and of itself, is not a bad thing. People simply disagree about the best way to solve a problem, and they advance positions that eventually develop into legislation, and then we vote for those candidates who most closely align with the legislation we prefer. At its best, politics is a nonviolent process by which people work through their disagreements. The problem arises when different viewpoints become hardened to the point that the division sparked (or, more often, fueled) by disagreement becomes a permanent feature of the society. When this happens, politics becomes less a process of working through disagreement and more a battle to defeat the opponent. People then begin to respond to questions out of a fixed ideological framework rather than examining the actual substance of questions.

Unfortunately, religion lends itself to such division quite readily. The texts, practices, doctrines, and theologies of the Christian tradition are full of language of division: elect and damned, righteous and unrighteous, good and evil, those welcome to the communion table and those not welcome, those who may be ordained to ministry and those who may not be. As we consider methods for bringing faith to bear on politics, we need to begin by acknowledging the rhetoric and practices of our faith that lend themselves to the politics of division.

Fortunately, there are also texts, practices, doctrines, and theologies of the Christian tradition that speak of inclusion, equality, and relationship. To my mind, one particularly powerful antidote to the politics of division is the virtue of *agape*, understood as unconditional love. This virtue (which is not unique to the Christian tradition) makes no distinction between persons and thus prompts us to respond not to the division, but to the common humanity buried beneath it. Chapter 1 focuses on *agape* as "love in action" by considering related concepts found in nonviolent resistance for social change. I turn to this literature of nonviolent social change because it describes individuals who enter into heated sites of conflict and face verbal and physical abuse, yet relentlessly advocate for a cause without "violence of fist, tongue, or heart." In their particular contexts, Mahatma Gandhi, Martin Luther King, Jr., Thich Nhat Hanh, Desmond Tutu, and Dorothy Day—along with the countless volunteers who worked with them—transformed politics by exercising love in action, rather than furthering the politics of division.

The Rhetoric of Certitude

A second problematic feature of politics is that it privileges absolute statements over more nuanced or open-ended positions. As people disagree, debate, and lobby for votes, the complexities and ambiguities around positions recede into the background, leaving only rhetoric of certitude and simplicity. Effective advocacy and successful campaigns seem to require this language. Political candidates who talk about gray areas are perceived as wishy-washy, weak, or evasive. Advocating for a position against opponents who dogmatically present disagreeable views requires an equally dogmatic response. No one can compete in this political climate without employing the rhetoric of certitude.

Again, religion lends itself to this purpose quite well. Orthodoxies (right belief) of various kinds, for example, thrive on and maintain absolute distinctions between right and wrong doctrine. And, to be fair, one can say the same thing about orthopraxies (right action), an approach to faith with which I am much more sympathetic. Still, the distinctions are made as clearly as possible between right and wrong practice, defining the parameters for truly Christian behavior. At a minimum, some kind of absolute conviction seems to be a requirement of religious belonging: why be Christian if you are, for example, unsure about the uniqueness of Jesus Christ? Religion lends itself to the political rhetoric of certitude because it employs such language regularly in its texts, doctrines, statements, and practices. And, like the evasive politician, the questioning believer is received warily by religious institutions that perceive struggles with ambiguity as a sign of weak faith.

Fortunately, such absolutist tendencies in religion do not constitute the whole of the experience and practice of faith. Indeed, religious institutions themselves do not constitute the whole life of faith, which extends far beyond the tradition's institutionalized expression. In the experience and practices of faith, we find room for moral ambiguity and are even called to pay careful attention to it. Moral ambiguity is a feeling of tension, fragmentation, or uncertainty that persists as one wrestles with an ethical question and even after one has reached a conclusion or made a decision. A residue remains in the form of lingering questions, grief, and doubt. This is the very stuff of faith: the struggles related to deeply held commitments, the questions about one's own behavior or that of a group to which one has been loyal, and the tension we feel between our own good fortune and the misery of others. If we reduce the experience of faith to the absolutist expression often present in our religious institutions, we lose an opportunity to bring faith into politics in a transformative way. We conform our faith to the politics of certitude so that we can compete in the game rather than embodying a faith that might actually change the game.

The Divine Endorsement

A third troublesome feature of politics is that it seeks endorsement as a way to strengthen power. In the height of a campaign season, we see this most clearly as candidates seek and celebrate endorsements from influential people and from organizations representing different segments of society. For the most part, this is a rather benign practice. It may result in people voting according to endorsement rather than issues, but following the lead of an organization or individual who articulates one's interests and convictions is not antithetical to the democratic process. The problem really emerges when religion enters this mix, as it is poised to do. To put it most simply, religion appears to offer a divine endorsement.

Religious history is filled with examples of political leaders who were draped with God's mantel by religious leaders who also benefited from a cozy relationship with the state. President George W. Bush is certainly not the first to claim that his policies align with Providence, nor will he be the last. And religious communities advocating for public policies that are consonant with their religious commitments regularly make the argument that *this* is God's politics.

Now, as indicated earlier, I think that Christians should seek public policies that are consonant with religious commitments, lest faith become devoid of all social import and public meaning. There is a social message at the heart of the Christian tradition, and Christians cannot embody that message without attending to the public policies and social institutions that govern people's lives. But, given the history of religious endorsement for violence, tyranny, and injustice and given the political hunger for endorsement, we must be exceedingly careful about the ways we seek and articulate consonance between religious conviction and public policy.

I believe that the strongest antidote to divine endorsement is theological humility, which begins with the honest admission that we do not know the mind of God. Our knowledge is limited and partial. What we see, even through the eyes of faith, is conditioned by where we stand. So, my understanding or interpretation of God's will, for example, is not the same thing as God's will. It is my understanding or my interpretation, and this holds true for everyone. The political context tempts us toward the strongest of theological statements, especially when our opponents are making them. Theological bravado serves the rhetoric of politics well. The antidote is theological humility, which I will describe in the third chapter as a posture that (1) admits limitations of knowledge and partiality of perspective, (2) explicitly and deliberately practices hermeneutics, and (3) remains transparent about faith commitments and accountable to other sources of knowledge. Theological humility is the most appropriate posture for faith in a pluralistic society because it inhibits religious authoritarianism.

Conformity or Transformation?

Unconditional love, attention to moral ambiguity, and a posture of theological humility are not ingredients for political success in the United States. These three things are not politically effective in the narrow sense of contributing to a legislative or electoral victory. The driving concern of this book is the instrumental use of religion in politics and the ways in which our religious expression in the public sphere betrays the best intentions of our faith.

The Christian mandate to inclusive love is betrayed by a religious expression that adopts the rhetoric of division. The necessary presence of doubt and contrition in the life of faith is betrayed by a religious expression that conforms to a rhetoric of certitude and self-righteousness. And the delicate interplay between reason and faith is betrayed by religious expression that uses theological bravado to offer the divine endorsement.

These three commitments—love, ambiguity, humility—may not be politically effective in a narrow sense, but they are politically effective in the much broader sense of carrying the potential to transform politics in positive ways. When we bring faith into the public square, we must embody love in action because unconditional love insists on a relationship that runs deeper than division. We must attend to moral ambiguity because acknowledging and working with the gray areas increases the chances of finding common ground with others and makes some form of reconciliation more likely. And we must practice theological humility because it is the best way to make faith commitments a part of a political conversation without imposing them on other people. In other words, theological humility enables religion to be a participant in pluralistic, democratic discourse and thus contributes to a relationship between religion and politics that is constructively and mutually critical, rather than either antagonistic or instrumental. I not only advocate these commitments as corrective to the instrumental use of religion in politics, but I also believe in their inherent value and potential to transform the process.

I do not envision an immediately apparent transformation, but the furthering of an ongoing transformative process. Transformation does not occur when we repeat the same patterns of behavior; rather it requires that we risk doing something in a new way. Thus, we further the process of transformation by continuing to disrupt patterns of behavior. What difference would it make if Christians entered the public square not as a force for further division, but as embodiments of a love that insists upon relationship? I think it would further the process of "transforming the human race into the human family."[1] What difference would it make if Christians would speak about our convictions *and* our uncertainties related to public policies? I think it would further the process of transforming ideologically separated people into human beings with views that sometimes diverge and sometimes overlap, thus making dialogue, compromise, and reconciliation more possible. What difference would it make if Christians were honest about the limitations of our knowledge and the processes of interpretation involved in faithful discernment? I think it would further the process of transforming the public role of religion from that of imperial authority to participant in discourse, with the right of voice and the responsibility of openness to critical engagement from others.

We have the opportunity to contribute to such transformation every time that we engage someone whose views differ from our own. These engagements may take place in formal or structured interactions such as town hall debates or public forums on contentious issues. They may also take place as activists encounter their opponents in the context of a march, vigil, petition drive, or canvassing campaign. But these opportunities also arise every day in workplaces, at ball fields, in check-out lines, and on airplanes. The "public square" is not a neatly circumscribed area that we enter only at a specified time for a pre-planned discussion. Much more often, we find ourselves thrust into the public square by a comment or question related to a social issue. My use of the phrase, public square, denotes a circumstance more than a place, a circumstance marked by a plurality of views and by discussion of issues that affect people beyond the discussants. In this sense, the public square is everywhere, even though we are frequently surprised by its appearance around us. Whether we plan our entry into a structured public space or we find ourselves thrust into these pluralistic social debates, we must carefully attend to the form of our engagement with the people and issues we meet there.

When I preached the sermon that gave rise to the email mentioned earlier, I took Matthew 5:13-16 as my text. The familiar passage from Jesus' Sermon on the Mount is a call to distinctiveness—to remain "salty" rather than become bland, to reflect a light rather than become covered or snuffed out. There are certainly deeds required of us to remain salty and well-lit,[2] but I take this passage to also direct our attention to the spirit in which we act. I do not believe that the call to distinctiveness requires withdrawal from society, politics, and culture. But I do think that we are called to behave within these structures in light of a story that extends beyond them. We must not allow religious and political differences to smother awareness of our common humanity. We must not allow the rhetoric of certitude and unequivocal posturing to bury self-critical reflection and empathy for others. And we must not allow the light of a gracious and loving God to be hidden under the bushel of antagonistic politics. All of this means that we must attend to the form of the faith that we bring into the public square. In this process of transformation, form is as important as content.

CHAPTER ONE

Love

With this chapter, we begin to turn our attention from the substance of the debates to their form. Chapters 1 through 3 make three recommendations regarding the form of progressive Christian political engagement: (1) that it should take the shape of love in the public square, (2) that it should attend honestly and deliberately to moral ambiguity, and (3) that it should practice theological humility. This chapter draws on guidance from the history of nonviolent action to argue that love must accompany Christian political engagement, and to describe this love in action.

Love, as a subject in Christian ethics, has a long history as one would imagine, given its primacy as one of the three theological virtues. It has, moreover, received particularly intense scholarly scrutiny since Anders Nygren published *Agape and Eros* in the 1930s.[1] Around the same time, Reinhold Niebuhr began to articulate the distinction he sees between love and justice, a distinction that appears in various forms throughout his life's work.[2] Gene Outka, ethics professor at Yale University, has also shaped this discussion with his systematic treatment, *Agape: An Ethical Analysis*.[3] With the rise of liberation movements, the self-sacrificial aspect of *agape* came under critical scrutiny. In the 1970s, Roman Catholic ethicist Margaret Farley joined other feminists to emphasize love as mutuality and equality rather than self-sacrifice.[4]

It is important to know that there is a history of scholarship on the ethics of love. However, the resources informing this chapter primarily come from the history of nonviolent resistance, where we find descriptions and examples of love persisting in the crucible of conflict. Mahatma Gandhi, Martin Luther King, Jr., Thich Nhat Hanh, Desmond Tutu, and Dorothy Day provide us with helpful language for and practices of love in the context of struggles for social change. The following pages provide a brief description of five related concepts, one from each figure: *ahimsa*, *agape*, interbeing, *ubuntu*, and personalism. It is helpful to think in terms of a Venn diagram, a series of overlapping circles.

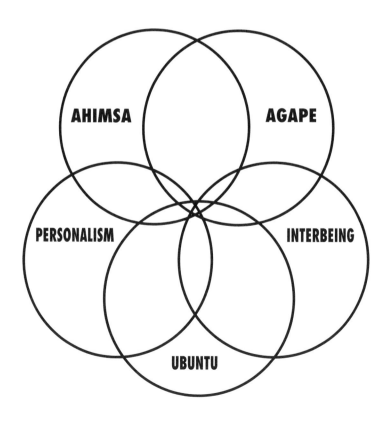

Each concept has its own context, meaning, history, and religious tradition, but there is also a common area that provides additional texture to the concept of love in the context of political engagement.

Unconditional Love as a Starting Point

I believe that Christians should engage politics with a love that risks not being reciprocated, an unconditional love for all, a love that makes no distinction between friend and enemy. This is not a universal argument for unconditional love as the highest form of love in every context. It is an argument for the necessity of *agape* in situations of heated political conflict where we must learn to confront one another without hatred. As I will argue more fully later in this chapter, I recommend this form of love in politics because I believe we are fundamentally related in such ways that your benefit is not wholly distinct from mine, and because I believe that this form of love has the potential to transform our politics and our societies in positive ways. I find myself nodding to the truthfulness and importance of *agape* as described by Gene Outka:

> *Agape* then includes unilateral efforts to establish and enhance personal relations marked by closeness and social relations marked by concord. It does not await, anticipate, or demand a response in kind, though it desires and hopes for such a response, and takes actual attainment as the fruition it seeks. It will, moreover, strive for reconciliation that forsakes negative equivalence: 'When reviled, we bless; when persecuted, we endure; when slandered, we try to conciliate' (1 Corinthians 4:12b-13 [RSV]). The refusal to make reciprocity a condition for care about another's well-being points likewise toward universal love.[5]

I do not think that a love that refuses "to make reciprocity a condition for care" is the only form of Christian love. But I do think it is an essential posture for Christians in the public square.

In her reflections on the suspension of human rights and civil liberties for those suspected of terrorism, philosopher Judith Butler writes, "Whether or not we continue to enforce a universal conception of human rights at moments of outrage and incomprehension, precisely when we think that others have taken themselves out of the human community as we know it, is a test of our very humanity."[6] I feel the same way about the commitment to unconditional love in the context of heated political debate. My ability to care for the well-being of the very person whose views threaten the people and values I hold dear is a test of my humanity and my discipleship. We are not called to discipleship only in private places or only when it is politically effective. Discipleship requires that we reflect the light of a gracious and loving God. We cannot do this when we place that light under the bushel of political division and public antagonism.

To take it a step further, I am convinced that means and ends are related, to the point that we cannot realize a beloved community with less than loving means. Deep in my own faith and family tradition is the pietist conviction that connects action with character formation: I become what I do. The study of nonviolence convinced me that this sense of individual character formation also holds true on larger, social scales. We, as communities, become what we do.

Gandhi put it this way: "They say 'means are after all [just] means.' I would say 'means are after all everything.' As the means, so the end."[7] As Gandhian scholar Rex Ambler explains, the connection between means and ends "exemplified the fundamental strategy of Gandhian peacemaking, which was *to embody the goals to be struggled for in the conduct of the struggle itself.*"[8] Like Gandhi, King preached the connection between means and ends, adding that hateful acts contribute to hate in the universe.[9] In his account of the Montgomery bus boycott, King writes:

> In my weekly remarks as president [of the Montgomery Improvement Association], I stressed that the use of violence in our struggle would be both impractical and immoral. To meet hate with retaliatory hate would do nothing but intensify the existence of evil in the universe. Hate begets hate; violence begets violence; toughness begets a greater toughness. We must meet the forces of hate with the power of love; we must meet physical force with soul force.[10]

This connection between means and ends is so important because we create the future through our present actions. If we want a less violent future, we must act less violently in the present. Repeating behavior does not make transformation possible. Transformation requires that we disrupt the pattern. If I respond to hate in kind, then I foreclose the possibility of a new opportunity in the future. But if I respond to hate with love, then I have introduced a new possibility; I have created a space for love to grow.

I want to stress that unconditional love is not the only form of love suited to the public square, in my view. But in these situations of intense conflict, we must begin with agape because it functions as a negative limit: No matter what, we refuse to hate and to dehumanize those whom we confront. In the predominantly Buddhist context of Vietnam, Thich Nhat Hanh pointed to non-duality and interbeing as the concepts that could transform a society splitting so violently along ideological lines. In India, Gandhi called on *ahimsa* as an ancient precept to counter the divisive violence of imperialism and inter-religious warfare. In our contemporary U.S. context marked by ideological division that is exacerbated in campaign seasons, Christians should practice a form of love that confronts without hatred.

In order to give texture to the call to love in the context of political engagement, I begin with a review of the meaning and role of *agape* in the writings of Martin Luther King, Jr. I then draw on four other concepts as well. *Ahimsa* is a precept from Hindu, Jain, and Buddhist traditions that means, at a minimum, not to cause injury to another living thing.[11] But, as we will see, it also calls for an "over-flowing love for all."[12] *Agape* and *ahimsa* overlap to issue a clear call for renouncing violence in thought, word, and deed, and returning hatred with love. Now, how do we do this? How do we renounce anger? How do we stop harboring ill will, let alone act with love toward people whose views not only are disagreeable, but indeed threaten some of our core values? Continuing our survey of nonviolent resistance, we find three further concepts that help to answer these questions because they underscore the reality of interrelatedness, and insist on the inherent dignity and worth of every person.

Interbeing is a word created by Thich Nhat Hanh as the best approximation of the Vietnamese words, *Tiep Hien*. Thich Nhat Hanh founded the Buddhist Order of *Tiep Hien* in Vietnam in the mid-1960s. In this order we have another example of a religious community, forged in the crucible of conflict, committed to overcoming violence and ideological division with a commitment to, in this case, interbeing: "I am; therefore you are. We interare."[13] Interbeing is grounded in the Buddhist notion of non-duality, which means that no single thing exists apart from other things. Separateness is illusory; "there is no such thing as an individual," writes Thich Nhat Hanh.[14] Archbishop Desmond Tutu's use of the African concept of *ubuntu* offers a similar picture of an interrelated human family. Like all of the concepts referenced here, *ubuntu* has a complex meaning that stretches far beyond the sliver I examine. But, there is present within this broad concept an idea that overlaps with interbeing to emphasize the depth of human interrelatedness. "My humanity is caught up, is inextricably bound up, in yours."[15] Interbeing and *ubuntu* deepen the hue of human connection and issue a clear call to perceive and act according to our relatedness to one another. Finally, I turn to the Catholic Worker movement and personalism, a concept that has a complex and broad history as well as a helpful overlap with *agape*. One central tenet of personalism is that we affirm the dignity of every person; or in explicitly Christian language, we seek the face of Christ (or that of God) in every person. After an introduction to each term, I offer a series of practices for love in the context of divisive politics.

Renounce Violence in Thought, Word, and Deed

After graduating from Crozer Seminary and completing doctoral work at Boston University, Martin Luther King, Jr. accepted a position as pastor of Dexter Avenue Baptist Church in Montgomery, Alabama. During his second year in Montgomery, Rosa Parks refused to relinquish her seat on the bus, and King found himself (at age 26) at the forefront of civil disobedience. In his account of the Montgomery bus boycott in *Stride Toward Freedom*, King describes the emergence of the "basic philosophy that guided the movement."

> This guiding principle has since been referred to variously as nonviolent resistance, noncooperation, and passive resistance. But in the first days of the protest none of these expressions was mentioned; the phrase most often heard was "Christian love." It was the Sermon on the Mount, rather than a doctrine of passive resistance, that initially inspired the Negroes of Montgomery to dignified social action. It was Jesus of Nazareth that stirred the Negroes to protest with the creative weapon of love. As the days unfolded, however, the inspiration of Mahatma Gandhi began to exert its influence. I had come to see early that the Christian doctrine of love operating through the Gandhian method of nonviolence was one of the most potent weapons available to the

Negro in his struggle for freedom. . . . Nonviolent resistance had emerged as the technique of the movement, while *love stood as the regulating ideal*. In other words, Christ furnished the spirit and motivation, while Gandhi furnished the method.[16]

King is not speaking of love in a sentimental or affectionate sense; thus the insistence on *agape* rather than *eros* or *philia*. *Agape* is "disinterested love," meaning that it seeks not one's own good, but the good of another, and does not distinguish between "worthy and unworthy people."[17] It "is an entirely 'neighbor-regarding concern for others,' which discovers the neighbor in every [person] it meets."[18] King understood *agape* as a cohesive factor in even the most divided societies. "*Agape* is love seeking to preserve and create community. . . . *Agape* is a willingness to go to any length to restore community. . . . It is a willingness to forgive, not seven times, but seventy times seven to restore community."[19] Indeed, "agape is the only cement that can hold this broken community together."[20]

The story of King's "pilgrimage to nonviolence" includes an influential sermon by Howard University President Dr. Mordecai Johnson. Dr. Johnson had just returned from India and spoke at length about Mahatma Gandhi. King writes,

> His message was so profound and electrifying that I left the meeting and bought a half dozen books on Gandhi's life and works. Like most people, I had heard of Gandhi, but I had never studied him seriously. As I read I became deeply fascinated by his campaigns of nonviolent resistance. . . . As I delved deeper into the philosophy of Gandhi my skepticism concerning the power of love gradually diminished, and I came to see for the first time its potency in the area of social reform. . . . Love, for Gandhi, was a potent instrument for social and collective transformation. It was in this Gandhian emphasis on love and nonviolence that I discovered the method for social reform that I had been seeking for so many months.[21]

Mahatma Gandhi's method was called, *satyagraha*, "the Force which is born of Truth and Love or Non-violence."[22] *Satya* means truth; *agraha* means firmness. The very first item in the 1930 code of discipline for those practicing *satyagraha* is: "Harbor no anger but suffer the anger of the opponent. Refuse to return the assaults of the opponent."[23] Gandhi then explains the commitment more fully:

> A *satyagrahi* must never forget the distinction between evil and the evil-doer. He must not harbour ill-will or bitterness against the latter. He may not even employ needlessly offensive language against the evil person, however unrelieved his evil might be. For it is an article of faith with every *satyagrahi* that there is no one so fallen in this world but can be converted by love. A *satyagrahi* will always try to overcome evil by good, anger by love, untruth by truth, *himsa* by *ahimsa*. There is no other way of purging the world of evil.[24]

Gandhi defines *ahimsa* as "a complete freedom from ill will and anger and hate and an overflowing love for all."[25] Like each of these five concepts discussed in this chapter, *ahimsa* is a broad and complex notion, and it comes from multiple religious traditions. Joan Bondurant describes *ahimsa* as "an ancient Hindu, Jain, and Buddhist ethical precept. The negative prefix 'a' plus 'himsa,' loosely meaning 'injury,' make up the word which is usually translated as non-violence. Yet *ahimsa* is eminently more than a negative notion."[26] As Gandhi writes, "Not to hurt any living thing is no doubt a part of *ahimsa*. But it is its least expression. The principle of *himsa* is hurt by every evil thought, by undue haste, by lying, by hatred, by wishing ill to anybody."[27] "Ahimsa really means that you may not offend anybody, you may not harbor an uncharitable thought even in connection with one who may consider himself to be your enemy."[28]

We can see King's integration of *agape* and *ahimsa* most concretely in the language of the Commitment Card that participants in the Birmingham Campaign were asked to sign. Regardless of the hatred and violence visited upon them, the protestors were committed to "walk and talk in the manner of love" and to "refrain from the violence of fist, tongue, or heart."[29] We find similar commitments among the list that constituted the Code of Discipline for Gandhi's campaign in 1930: (1) "Harbor no anger but suffer the anger of the opponent. Refuse to return the assaults of the opponent," (2) "Refrain from insults and swearing," and (3) if taken prisoner, behave in an exemplary manner.[30] The actions themselves are never intended to "defeat or humiliate the opponent, but to win his friendship and understanding."[31] To that end, each "attack is directed against forces of evil rather than against persons who happen to be doing the evil."[32] Nonviolent resistance aims to avoid "not only external physical violence but also internal violence of spirit. The nonviolent resister not only refuses to shoot his opponent but he *also refuses to hate him.*"[33] Thus, resisters practice methods that further the ultimate goal of reconciliation and transformation. For example, a student leader during the Civil Rights movement, Diane Nash, explains, "We used nonviolence as an expression of love and respect of the opposition, while noting that a *person* is never the enemy. The enemy is always attitudes, such as racism or sexism; political systems that are unjust; economic systems that are unjust—some kind of system or attitude that oppresses."[34]

This discipline is rooted in several core tenets, two of which we have now discussed, namely the foundational commitment to non-injury and to love, and the belief in the connection between means and ends. It is also grounded in awareness of relationship, as King explains. "In the final analysis, *agape* means a recognition of the fact that all life is interrelated. . . . If you harm me, you harm yourself."[35] Three further commitments reinforce this sense of connection to the opponent and buttress the practice with an affirmation of the dignity of every person.

Perceive the Connection with the Opponent

As mentioned earlier, Buddhist monk Thich Nhat Hanh founded the Order of Tiep Hien in Vietnam in the mid-1960s. He explains that this order "derives from the Zen School of Lin Chi, and is the forty-second generation of the school. It is a form of engaged Buddhism, Buddhism in daily life, in society, and not just in a retreat center."[36] In his introduction to *Interbeing*, Fred Eppsteiner elaborates on this history. "The Order was formed at a time when destruction in the name of supposedly irreconcilable 'isms' was painfully evident in Vietnam. Thich Nhat Hanh was acutely aware of the need for all people to overcome ideological divisiveness."[37] The meaning of the terms, *Tiep Hien*, captures this commitment to overcome such division. This purpose is seen even more clearly in the fourteen mindfulness trainings to which all members commit themselves, and we will discuss some of these shortly.[38]

Tiep and *hien* are Vietnamese words of Chinese derivation with meanings that are not easily translated. The overall sensibility, though, is of deep connectedness experienced in the present time. *Tiep* means "to be in touch with." And Thich Nhat Hanh explains that one strives to be in touch with "the reality of the world and the reality of the mind." "To be in touch with the reality of the world means to be in touch with everything that is around us in the animal, vegetal, and mineral realms." Regarding the reality of the mind, "When we discover our true mind, we are filled with understanding and compassion, which nourishes us and those around us as well."[39] *Tiep* also means "continuing," and Thich Nhat Hanh uses the image of a string to explain this. He writes, "To tie two strings together to make a longer string. It means extending and perpetuating the career of enlightenment that was started and nourished by the Buddhas and bodhisattvas who preceded us."[40]

Hien means "realizing," as in making our beliefs real in the world. Convictions are embodied; they find full expression in a transformed life. "Hien means not to dwell or be caught in the world of doctrines and ideas, but to bring and express our insights into real life."[41] Similarly, *hien* also means "making it here and now." This is no promise of a deferred paradise, leaving us to endure pain here. Rather, "The purpose is to have peace for ourselves and others right now, while we are alive and breathing."[42]

As I have struggled to understand these concepts, it has been helpful to see that they capture content and process, respectively. These terms offer an image of awakening or enlightenment and an affirmation that such enlightenment is possible here and now and can make a difference in our world. In an effort to convey the meaning of these concepts and make them more accessible to an English-speaking audience, Thich Nhat Hanh invented a new English word, interbeing, which he most succinctly explains this way: "I am, therefore you are. You are, therefore I am. That is the meaning of the word 'interbeing.' We interare."[43]

This definition of interbeing almost exactly matches one definition of *ubuntu* offered by Desmond Tutu. "It is to say, 'My humanity is caught up, is inextricably bound up, in yours.' We belong in a bundle of life. We say, 'A person is a person through other persons.'"[44] Like interbeing, *ubuntu* is a broad and complex concept with a rich religious and cultural history. Muendanyi Mahamba explains that "'Botho [Setswana word for *ubuntu*] means "our humanity"; it embraces everything which makes us human. *Botho* is essentially that which distinguishes humankind from the animal kingdom.'" He goes on to clarify the significant role that the community plays in shaping the person and assessing behavior. "In the spirit of *ubuntu* or of *botho*, a person is supposed to play the role which belongs to him or her in the community. Individual behaviour is judged in accordance with the community's expectations, which it considers correct."[45] One such behavior is "humanitarian activity" or, simply, helping one another. "The respect for human dignity, love in practice, relief from the weight of economic constraints due to costly burials, demonstration of solidarity—all this constitutes the deeper meaning of *ubuntu*."[46] Stanley Mogoba elaborates on this point:

> *Ubuntu* means to love and take care of others, ubuntu means to be nice to others, ubuntu means to be welcoming, ubuntu means to be fair and understanding, ubuntu means to be filled with compassion, ubuntu means to help those who are in distress, ubuntu means to be frank and honest, ubuntu means to have good manners. A country which practises ubuntu is the closest on earth to the kingdom of God.[47]

Archbishop Desmond Tutu's description of ubuntu includes examples of humanitarian activity, behavior that contributes to the well-being of the community. And he also reinforces the point that *ubuntu* is more than a set of behaviors; it is the conviction that community makes me human and that my humanity finds its fullest expression in community.

> *Ubuntu* is very difficult to render into a Western language. It speaks of the very essence of being human. When we want to give high praise to someone we say, "Yu, u nobuntu"; "Hey, so-and-so has ubuntu." Then you are generous, you are hospitable, you are friendly and caring and compassionate. You share what you have. . . . It is not, "I think therefore I am." It says rather: "I am human because I belong. I participate, I share."[48]

In his book, *Reconciliation: The Ubuntu Theology of Desmond Tutu*, Episcopal theologian Michael Battle provides a description and analysis of the ways in which *ubuntu* informed and sustained Tutu's anti-apartheid work. Tutu challenged the division and oppression of apartheid theologically by insisting "on the integrity of creation and the habitual recalling of our image of God (*imago Dei*) in the midst of human conflict."[49] Affirming the humanity of and the relationship between all persons, *ubuntu* theology "provides an invaluable perspective in which white and black people may see themselves as other than racial rivals."[50] Such conversion mitigates vengeance and makes reconciliation more possible by reminding us that we share a common humanity, which cannot find its fullest expression in division and hatred. In Tutu's words, "A person with *ubuntu* . . . know[s] that he or she belongs in a greater whole and is diminished when others are humiliated or diminished, when others are tortured or oppressed, or treated as if they were less than who they are."[51]

I recommend that we draw from interbeing and *ubuntu* to give sustenance to the commitment to love in situations of heated conflict. These rich concepts can function as nutrients in parched soil. The particular form of nutrition they provide is to deepen our awareness of interrelatedness. With all of our differences and underneath all of our hate-filled, divisive, and oppressive behaviors, we do indeed share a common humanity. We interare. The strength of these concepts comes not only from their meaning, but also from the contexts in which Thich Nhat Hanh and Desmond Tutu have asserted their truthfulness. Thich Nhat Hanh founded the Order of Tiep Hien when his society was being torn apart by ideological conflict. He asserted interbeing in the very crucible of conflict, as a way to make plain the illusions perpetuating the divide, and to map the path toward healing and peace. Thus, the first mindfulness training to which members of the order commit themselves is this:

> Aware of the suffering created by fanaticism and intolerance, we are determined not to be idolatrous about or bound to any doctrine, theory, or ideology, even Buddhist ones. Buddhist teachings are guiding means to help us learn to look deeply and to develop our understanding and compassion. They are not doctrines to fight, kill, or die for.[52]

Similarly, *ubuntu* is not an untested ideal. Rather, those who believe in *ubuntu* have lived it out in the contexts of racial hatred, legislated division, race-based oppression and violence, and religiously justified separation. A theology of *ubuntu* sustained Tutu's nonviolent approach to anti-apartheid work and his commitment to a process of truth-telling. In his discussion of the Truth and Reconciliation Commission, Tutu explains that this belief in a common humanity meant that the perpetrators of violence had to face the people whose humanity had been denied by legislation, violence, and supremacist ideologies. But it also meant that such a reckoning with wrongdoing could not, itself, dehumanize. Tutu and those who supported the TRC believed that this process of confession and amnesty restored humanity to the perpetrator as well as the victim. The TRC was designed, like nonviolent resistance campaigns, to reflect the hoped-for future, one in which freedom, equality, and full humanity were restored.[53]

In the lived expression of *ubuntu*, interbeing, *agape*, and *ahimsa*, we find a determined grip on commitments that one's society violates with abandon. This tenacity of conviction is buttressed by the belief that our present actions, thoughts, and speech shape the future. Giving up the commitments to "humanitarian activity," to affirming interrelatedness, and to love contributes to the foreclosure of a more humane and loving future. In his book titled

Reconciliation: Restoring Justice, South African theologian John W. De Gruchy writes, "Reconciliation is, if you like, a journey from the past into the future, a journey from estrangement to communion, or from what was patently unjust in search of a future that is just."[54] As Christians enter into the public square in the United States, we must maintain an awareness of the future that extends far beyond an election or legislative cycle. Our calling is to contribute to the transformation of society into a more peaceful, just, and caring place, and we can learn from those who worked urgently for change without losing sight of the future vision.

Affirm the Dignity of (Christ within) Each Person

Another commitment, forged and persisting in the context of difficult human relationships, is that of personalism. I gravitated toward this commitment the first time I read about it because of its similarity to the Quaker conviction that there is "that of God" in every person. This fundamental concept is, for me, the strongest argument for nonviolence in thought, word, and deed. I also discuss personalism here because it can serve as a kind of backstop in those moments when affirmation of relatedness to the opponent is truly hard to come by. Moreover, for those of us rooted in the western tradition, with its emphasis on individual dignity and human rights, personalism might be something we can more readily employ to sustain our loving practice than an awareness of interrelatedness. So, I offer this concept as one more way to shore up our love, one more commitment to sustain and nourish love in places and moments when it is, honestly, the last thing we feel.

The philosophy of personalism became a foundational commitment of the Catholic Worker movement from the start, thanks to the influence of co-founder Peter Maurin. When the "penny paper" first appeared in 1933, Maurin wrote the statement, "What the Catholic Worker Believes," the first line of which reads, "The Catholic Worker believes in the gentle personalism of traditional Catholicism." And seventy years later, this commitment remains front and center. "The Aims and Means of the Catholic Worker Movement" includes a paragraph on personalism,

> a philosophy which regards the freedom and dignity of each person as the basis, focus and goal of metaphysics and morals. In following such wisdom, we move away from a self-centered individualism toward the good of the other. This is to be done by taking personal responsibility for changing conditions, rather than looking to the state or other institutions to provide impersonal 'charity.' We pray for a Church renewed by this philosophy and for a time when all those who feel excluded from participation are welcomed with love, drawn by the gentle personalism Peter Maurin taught.[55]

The philosophy of personalism that Peter Maurin brought into the movement was much broader than its expression within the Catholic Worker. In the North American Protestant tradition, United Methodist Borden Parker Bowne shaped the philosophy of personalism during his thirty years at Boston University at the end of the nineteenth century.[56] However, the strain of personalism that informed the Catholic Worker came with Maurin from French Catholic philosophers, primarily Jacques Maritain and Emmanuel Mounier. In his text on these two thinkers, Joseph Amato offers the broadest definition of personalism as a starting point:

> In its broadest sense, Personalism is a diverse intellectual movement of the twentieth century. In part, it belongs to no one school; and in part it belongs to everyone who believes man is a personal and communal being who is mortally endangered by his own political, social, economic, and ideological creations.

Anyone, in fact, who in the name of man's worth seeks simulta-
neously to save man from isolation and tyranny, from the furies
of individualism and collectivism, can consider himself, if he
wishes, a Personalist. Personalism, defined in this loose sense,
includes a whole array of men and movements who, without offi-
cial program, are committed to man's transcendence and are the
enemies of all individuals, ideas, societies, and states that deny
man the needs of his body, the dignity of his spirit, the presence
and sustenance of a true human community.[57]

Maurin not only introduced the philosophy through discussion and
education; he also seems to have embodied it to such an extent that
he brought it into the movement in an incarnational way. In her
autobiography, Dorothy Day wrote about him this way:

He aroused in you a sense of your own capacities for work, for
accomplishment. He made you feel that you and all [people] had
great and generous hearts with which to love God. If you once
recognized this fact in yourself you would expect and find it in
others. "The art of human contacts," Peter called it happily. But
it was seeing Christ in others, loving the Christ you saw in others. Greater than this, it was having faith in the Christ in others
without being able to see Him.[58]

In his account of the Catholic Worker Movement, *Breaking
Bread*, Mel Piehl explains that Dorothy Day explicitly connected
personalism and love: "As Day came to interpret it for her followers, Maurin's radical Gospel personalism meant, above all, making
'Christian love' the foundation of social existence. True love
required, first of all, taking responsibility for one's self, then developing 'love in action' in service to one's immediate neighbors, and
then transforming society at large through the power of this love."[59]
The love so deeply connected to personalism is a kind of love in
action that pulls the workers into direct engagement with those in
need. The emphasis is on people helping people, responding to the

needs of a person in a way that respects dignity. "The personalist philosophy offered by Day and Maurin did not expect change through and in social and political institutions, but rather looked for the creative change in individuals as they elevated the Christian precept of active love to a place of practice primary in their daily lives."[60]

Our political activism must not neglect "the art of human contacts."[61] And by this, I do not mean networking and collaborating in an instrumental sense, where we establish relationships in order to further an interest. I mean that we must supplement our political activism in the public square with person-to-person contact with those on the other side of an issue. And we must forge these relationships with the goal of understanding, not conversion. In *A Moral Creed for All Christians*, Roman Catholic ethicist Daniel C. Maguire draws on Thomas Aquinas to offer this description of love in action. "Love is a unifying force, a fusion of vitalities. But solids cannot be blended together so love promotes union through the melting of barriers. It does so without squelching individuality. True love accentuates our differences as it bonds us into a fruitful union and is a boon to both lover and beloved."[62] The personalist practices of the Catholic Worker movement illustrate this process and teach us about the power (and unpredictability) of authentic interaction.

Additional Lessons about Love

I have stressed the breadth of these concepts to make clear that *ahimsa*, interbeing, *ubuntu*, and personalism are not synonymous with *agape*. These commitments overlap in ways that deepen our understanding of unconditional love and fortify its practice. In addition to contributing texture to the meaning of *agape*, these concepts and the people who practice them refute several false assumptions about unconditional love in situations of conflict: that it is impossible to practice, requires acquiescence and unity, and glorifies self-sacrifice. In the shared commitments of Gandhi and King, we see examples of a discipline of love that renounces violence in thought, word, and deed—or fist, tongue, and heart—even when one has such violence visited upon him or her. This is love in action, unconditional love working for justice. These leaders, and the thousands of volunteers who have practiced nonviolent methods ever since, testify to the possibility of confrontation without hatred. It is absolutely possible to engage the opponent in a public space of heated conflict without exhibiting and feeling hatred. It is not easy, but it is possible. The public spaces are not conducive to loving speech and behavior, but they cannot prohibit their expression.

Nonviolent resistance also demonstrates that unconditional love does not require acquiescence or capitulation. For years, Christian nonviolent activists have insisted that Jesus' call to love the enemy and to resist not the evildoer does not mandate acquiescence in the face of injustice or malevolence. Walter Wink gave this formal expression over twenty years ago in his description of "Jesus' third way" of nonviolent resistance.[63] I situate my recommendation for unconditional love in this trajectory of people who have practiced confrontation without hatred. I cannot overemphasize this point: mine is not a call for agreement or even for unity. It is a call to practice love in our dealings with one another, confrontational as they may be. We must learn to challenge each other without denying our common humanity and to perceive our deep interrelatedness without denying our differences. My goal is not to end political and religious disagreement; it is to establish the bottom line of nonviolence in thought, word, and deed.

Agape does not require unity; quite the contrary. *Agape* finds its fullest expression in sites of disunity, where it refuses to hate and refuses to wish or inflict harm. Interbeing and *ubuntu* supplement this commitment and practice by pointing to the depth of human interrelatedness. Whether or not we agree, we are connected to one another. The work is not so much overcoming difference as it is unearthing the common humanity buried beneath it. The proposal is both radical—in the sense of going deep, to the roots—and modest, that we practice confrontation without hatred, that we challenge one another without denying our common humanity.

This sense of deep relationship also challenges a dichotomous view of persons that prompts us to see other-regard as something wholly distinct from self-concern. Such a dichotomy places us in a zero sum game, where we must choose to take care of ourselves or to advance the good of another. We fall into this trap every time we take self-denial to be the measure of love. I do not agree that love is only virtuous if it has no benefit to us whatsoever, as long as it is performed with pure attention to the needs of the other as utterly apart from self-concern. Unconditional love is not a good thing *because* it entails self-sacrifice; such thinking makes self-sacrifice an ultimate value, an end to be pursued via *agape* among other things. Responding to hatred with love; affirming relationship with those who defile us; seeking the humanity within those who dehumanize us—these practices prevent our society from deteriorating into intractable violent conflict. These practices benefit all of us. I recommend *agape* because it has the potential to transform the world I care about into a less violent and more just place. Awareness of relationship—rather than a preoccupation with self-denial—sustains practices of unconditional love. My humanity is wrapped up in yours.

One of many helpful aspects of this conviction is that it liberates us from a preoccupation with self-sacrifice and from the resentments that accrue as we keep track of unreciprocated giving. I am risking a love that will not be reciprocated because I want my childlren to experience more community than division. I am practicing love because I want them to be able to work for justice without being consumed by hatred. These practices shift attention away from the extent of my giving and to the well-being of the community, to our shared bundle of life, and to the process that we are furthering.

Practicing Love in Conflict

In the wake of such material, concerns inevitably arise about practicality. "Sure, these superhuman heroes of nonviolence could do this, but I can't." I think it is true that these people were/are truly extraordinary *and* that such a comment is a cop-out. The space between these exemplars and our own sense of ability is not a chasm, but an open field for striving and practice. It is also an area that these figures acknowledged and a place where they labored. For example, Thich Nhat Hanh explains that even vegetarians ingest microorganisms in the water in which they boil their vegetables. "We cannot be completely nonviolent, but by being vegetarian, we are going in the direction of nonviolence. If we want to head north, we can use the North Star to guide us, but it is impossible to arrive at the North Star. Our effort is only to proceed in that direction."[64] It is in that spirit of striving, of heading toward the North Star, that the following practices are offered.

Martin Luther King's language of love as "the regulating ideal" is also very helpful here. References to ideals tend to precipitate a series of questions related to their "mode of application," in James Gustafson's language. Are we expected to conform ourselves and reality to the ideal? Or is the expectation less, such that we identify "compromises that [we] can live with, or approximations with which [we] can be satisfied"? Gustafson is correct in that utilizing language of ideals introduces "a sliding scale of judgment."[65] However, all of these questions assume a dualistic worldview that needs to be challenged. That is, concerns about conformity, approximation, and compromise assume two fixed realms, one in which ideals are possible and one in which they are not. If we see ourselves as involved in a process rather than stuck in a paradox, then we become more focused on the ways in which this immediate action determines the range of possibilities in the next moment. To speak of love as a regulating ideal makes beautiful sense in this framework. We regulate something in terms of its direction and its intensity; thus, a regulating ideal informs an ongoing process, a movement, or a series of actions, giving them direction and determining their intensity. As a regulating ideal, love directs and measures my action. The ideal itself never gets compromised; rather, it remains intact to provide direction and assessment of my choices. Each moment affords me the opportunity to practice love.

While working on this chapter, I attended a meeting at my church. The purpose of the meeting was to review, as a community, the things we had learned in the many forums offered throughout the year and to address the question, "Now what?" What are we going to do with all of this information we have received about the war in Iraq, genocide in Darfur, global warming, violence in Los Angeles, the Israel/Palestine conflict . . . ? Our rector, Ed Bacon, presented an agenda of responsibilities related to these issues and then invited questions and comments about fulfilling these responsibilities in the coming year. The first question from the audience got right to the heart of this chapter: "How can we continue to work for peace and justice and still show compassion for those who are not there yet?" How do we practice love toward those with whom we disagree? In his response, Ed reminded us of the

Eucharistic liturgy, that we seek Christ in all whom we meet. "We *seek* Christ," he emphasized, "even when he is in deep, deep disguise." Seeking Christ or that of God or the inherent value and dignity in each person is ongoing work, and it is a practice of love, not just a preliminary step to it.

Conversation between Persons Who Disagree

This work cannot be done from a distance. We must practice love in proximity to the very people who test this commitment most thoroughly. One of the great lessons of the Catholic Worker movement is the value of direct engagement. Although Catholic Workers most often speak of direct engagement with the poor, we can extend their practice to those with whom we disagree. We might think about the Catholic Worker model of direct, person-to-person engagement as akin to citizen diplomacy. Rather than relying on diplomatic representatives to speak for us and to confront or negotiate with the other group, we forge relationships with its members ourselves. This kind of practice furthers true understanding not only of the group's stated positions, but of some individual expressions of and reasons for it. I know that the major spokespersons for progressive Christianity do not fully represent my views and my experiences. Why, then, do I think that the major spokespersons for the religious right fully represent the views of other individuals? In order to practice love, we need direct person-to-person engagement. We have to practice the "art of human contacts."[66]

In my experience, one of the first things to happen in such direct engagement is that I gain a better understanding of the other person's perspective. Understanding is *not* the same thing as agreement, but it does enable a relationship to exist. For example, a few years ago, workers at three major supermarkets in southern

California went on strike and those of us who supported the workers boycotted the stores. One evening, my husband and I were
invited to dinner at the house of some friends who are theologically
and politically more conservative than we are. After dinner, our
friend boasted about crossing the picket line in every one of the
three grocery stores that day. I took the bait immediately: "You did
not!" Thus began a long and somewhat tense conversation about
unions, wages, and economic disparity.

The second time that my friend made the same point—if the
wages aren't good enough at one job, find another one—it dawned
on me that he and I have a radically different view of human freedom. He believes that individuals are fundamentally free to make
(or not make) their own way in the world; and I believe that we are
constrained in varying degrees by socio-economic structures. It was
a proverbial a-ha moment for me. I neither changed my view on
the grocery workers' strike nor condoned my friend's shopping practices that day, but I did leave with a much better understanding of
him as a person. Now, of course, I knew of this fundamental difference between conservative and liberal views of individuals, freedom, and social structures. But in that living room conversation,
what came to my mind was not the different points of view I have
read about. What came to me so clearly was an understanding of
our friend's take on the world, in a very personal sense.

As an ethics teacher, I deal with people's conflicting thoughts
and beliefs on a daily basis. And because I do this in an educational
setting—rather than, say, a political context or a courtroom—I
have the time to work in a dialogical way to facilitate discussion
about and understanding of the differences. Working with other
people's disagreements and through my own has fully convinced me
of the truthfulness of the Buddhist connection between love and
understanding. "Understanding and love are not two things, but

just one," writes Thich Nhat Hanh. He then tells a story about a brother who wakes up his sister so that she will not be late for school. She greets his good intention with incredible grouchiness, telling him to shut up and kicking him. He stomps off in anger. Then he remembers that she was coughing during the night and decides that she might be getting sick, and he is no longer angry. Hanh comments, "When you understand, you cannot help but love. You cannot get angry. To develop understanding, you have to practice looking at all living beings with the eyes of compassion. When you understand, you love."[67]

I am completely sympathetic with the skeptical response to this point. The description and the story illustrating it are way too simple to capture the difficult human emotions of anger and love. It also seems to overlook or deny something like righteous indignation, where I fully understand someone's point of view and feel angry because of it. I understand and share this impulse to reject the simple truth: "When you understand, you love." But I also know that I have had moments when this simple truth is the only explanation I have for my own dissipated anger. I should be clearer—I have had moments when my understanding dissipates my anger at the person voicing the viewpoint, even when my rage at the idea remains intact.

Once, in an introductory ethics course, I had an undergraduate student who expressed his view that "homosexuality is the one unforgivable sin." This is the kind of statement that causes me to seethe with rage. But this day, instead of responding immediately, I asked, "What makes you think that?" He replied, "Jesus never forgives homosexuals," prompting me to ask him if Jesus ever mentions homosexuals. When he said no, I suggested that Jesus might not mention homosexuality because he was not concerned about it. The student did not pivot in his view that day, though I hope that our exchange contributed to a process of change in his perspective.

What did change in that moment was my perception of him. I saw him as the product of a terrible religious education marked by incomplete biblical study, theology without an understanding of grace, and disregard for the people so swiftly condemned to hell. Asking what made him think that and discussing his response created space for a humanizing exchange. In the course of that exchange, I retained my anger at homophobia and at terrible religious education, but I also felt my anger at the student dissipate.

I keep this memory alive because it is so hard for me not to extend my hatred of homophobia to the people who express it. This exchange reminds me of the power of understanding to decrease hatred of persons when hatred of their views remains intact. Working to understand a point of view with which we completely disagree is a practice of love. Doing this work in a dialogical way with people who hold disagreeable—even offensive—views helps not only to increase understanding of positions but also to maintain relationship with persons.

Affirming the Humanity and Seeking the Christ in the Other

Understanding a person's point of view contributes to the process of love, but does not complete it. The models of nonviolent resistance and the *agape* commandment itself call us to do more than understand the other point of view. We are actually called to love the person who holds it. Understanding his or her point of view is a vital step in this process. Indeed, I think that love without such understanding is a rather shallow thing. However, if I work to understand the point of view without also working to love the person who expresses it, then I might as well be engaging a text as conversing with a person.

The humanizing effect that I mentioned above assumes that we engage the person as well as the idea, and it requires going beyond understanding the position to caring for the person who expresses it. Our work here is not only to understand the position but to seek the Christ in every person or to identify that of God in every person. This is the ongoing labor of a love that does not distinguish between friend and enemy: to affirm the goodness within and to will the well-being of *every* person. I do not pretend that this is easy; nor do I claim to accomplish it in my own life. But I do believe that this kind of deep love is the regulating ideal against which we must measure our interaction with others and toward which we must always strive.

I have written elsewhere about practicing the moral imagination, which I describe as that faculty that enables us to perceive deep connections running beneath social, ideological, religious, and political divisions.[68] We exercise the moral imagination in a variety of ways. Thich Nhat Hanh, for example, describes a meditative practice of imagining the person (whom we are trying to love) as a child. Once we have a picture of that person as a child in our mind, then we recall the feeling we have for a child we know and love, and we work to extend that kind of love toward the imagined child and finally to his or her grown-up self. We engage this meditative practice repeatedly so that the feeling of love might finally take hold somewhere and begin to grow. And we return to this practice each time that an encounter with (or even a thought about) the person causes hatred to take hold again.

I do not regularly practice this particular meditation, but I do a similar thing. When I am confronted with someone who makes my blood boil, I say to myself: This is someone's child. In the time it takes for me to think them, these four words have the effect of quelling my anger a bit and opening my heart a bit. I do not fully understand why or how this works, but I think it has something to do with calling to mind my own children and my concern for their well-being. There is some mysterious power in that and in the ability to extend that feeling of concern to this other person's child, who is right now offending me. This simple statement keeps me from wishing harm to the person and, on my better days, begins a process of willing his or her well-being.

It is important that each of us find that simple statement or that image that enables us to check hatred in the middle of a heated exchange. This will be different for everyone, I assume. The trick is to find something powerful enough to mitigate hatred. I think that something this powerful is most likely to be tied to your deepest love. Where do you love most deeply? And what can you bring from that locus of deep love into the site of conflict? Identifying this thing and employing it at the necessary time are practices of love.

Self-purification and Ongoing Preparation

The process of redirecting our anger from person to point of view and to policy involves another kind of ongoing work. For this reason, movements for nonviolence incorporate a step sometimes referred to as self-purification.[69] In his book about the Birmingham campaign, Martin Luther King identifies self-purification as one of four steps in a nonviolent action campaign, the others being fact-finding, negotiation, and direct action.[70] The stage of self-purification included training primarily in the form of "socio-dramas designed to prepare the demonstrators for some of the challenges they could expect to face." The purpose was to prepare participants to respond to these challenges "with the nonviolent creed in action: to resist without bitterness; to be cursed and not reply; to be beaten and not hit back."[71] Self-purification is not performed only once, but rather revisited as one needs to rededicate himself or herself to the commitments and practices of nonviolence.

The Gandhian process of preparation is called *swaraj*, the first two points of which seem particularly important to this discussion.

> Firstly, we must acquire greater mastery over ourselves and secure an atmosphere of perfect calm, peace and good will. We must ask forgiveness for every unkind word thoughtlessly uttered or unkind deed done to anyone. . . . Secondly, we must still further cleanse our hearts, and we Hindus and Moslems must cease to suspect one another's motives, and we should believe ourselves to be incapable of wrongdoing one another.[72]

I believe that dialogue with those with whom we disagree contributes to this preparation or purification process. Indeed, in my experience, relinquishing hate is better accomplished in dialogue with someone on the other side than in solitude or in the company of like-minded people. Such dialogue may not be possible in the public square, but it can certainly be practiced before and after we enter that public space so that we maintain our commitments to love and rededicate ourselves to confrontation without hatred.

I want to emphasize that this movement from preparation/purification to action is not a linear process. For the health of the participants and the movement, it is often necessary to return to the purification/preparation stage and revisit the commitment and resources for nonviolence. Renouncing such anger takes rigorous spiritual practice, as Gandhi explains.

> By a long course of prayerful discipline I have ceased for over forty years to hate anybody. I know this is a big claim. . . . But I can and do hate evil wherever it exists. I hate the system of Government the British people have set up in India. I hate the domineering manner of Englishmen as a class in India. I hate the ruthless exploitation of India even as I hate from the bottom of my heart the hideous system of untouchability for which millions

of Hindus have made themselves responsible. But I do not hate the domineering Englishmen as I refuse to hate the domineering Hindus. I seek to reform them in all the loving ways that are open to me. My non-cooperation has its root not in hatred, but in love.[73]

The ongoing work of self-purification also means that we continue to examine ourselves and the systems in which we participate. Where do we see remnants of hatred in our practices and speech? Where do we find behavior and rhetoric that need to be re-evaluated?

Reconsidering Our Language

A few years after the living room debate over unions and wages, our friends dropped by our house one afternoon. In preparation for writing this book, I had been reading Bob Edgar's book, *Middle Church*, which is subtitled *Reclaiming the Moral Values of the Faithful Majority from the Religious Right*.[74] The book was in open view on a table in the living room, and our friend noticed it as he passed by. He paused, picked up the book, and said something to this effect: "Oh, now we've stolen your values and you have to get them back?" The way he personalized the question (we've done this to you?) gave me pause, and his question has remained with me as I listen to progressive Christians in the public square. We do regularly use this language of theft and retrieval. "They have taken our faith, and we must get it back." Some even say that "the religious right has hijacked Jesus."[75] There is some truth in such language insofar as the religious right puts itself forward as Christ's representative on public matters, defining what the Christian and non-Christian positions are. But surely we can challenge selective use of the Bible, theological oversights, and insensitivity to the implications of one's beliefs for others, rather than calling conservative Christians thieves and hijackers. At a minimum, such language betrays a commitment to "resist without bitterness." It also reflects and exacerbates our own feelings of fear and vulnerability.

I do not deny the legitimacy of these feelings. The platform of the religious right in our country scares me. It threatens my freedom as a woman; it denigrates the love, commitment, and personhood of my gay and lesbian friends; it makes an idol of American military, economic, and political power in the world; it draws cruel distinctions between those worthy of charity and hospitality and those unworthy; and it flatly denies my relationship with God and invalidates my understanding of and commitment to Christian discipleship. This is an infuriating situation; my blood pressure rises just typing the words. But the religious right has not taken my faith. They have not hijacked Jesus. I still hold my faith, and neither Jesus of Nazareth nor the Christ of faith can be held hostage by anyone. What they have done is to misrepresent the teachings of Christianity in the public square and to worsen the error by claiming that their misrepresentation is the only true version of the faith. I disagree with their views and reject their claim to be *the* Christian voice in politics, but I do not believe that they have taken anything of mine. Believing this enables me to enter the fray in order to articulate different Christian commitments and advocate for public policies that most fully embody them. We need to understand our work in the public square as something more constructive than antagonistic. Our primary task is to articulate and advocate for a more just and peaceable world, not to take back our faith.

This movement away from antagonism requires, among other things, that we see the broader context of our interaction, namely God's inclusive love.[76] In our fighting, we lose sight of this larger narrative and even purposefully disregard it. We become consumed by the immediate context of a polarizing debate and claim that God affiliates with our side alone. Our language of theft and retrieval, our feelings of fear and vulnerability, and our antagonistic and divisive behavior do not reflect the spirit of God who embraces us all. God's grace and love are not subject to *our* debates; rather, we are all subject to God's grace and love. Remembering this larger context does not prevent disagreement, nor should it. But it can and should enable us to disagree without the violence of thought, word, and deed.

It is exceedingly difficult to recall this broader context at the moment when we are swept up in the anxieties and urgencies of a contentious debate. The history of nonviolent resistance teaches us that it is necessary to incorporate practices of meditation, prayer, self-purification, and reflection into our activism so that we can remain nonviolent. We must work to perceive relationship beneath division; we must *seek* the Christ in others; we must find strength to affirm the dignity of the person who attacks us. Before we enter the fray, while we are immersed in it, and after we emerge from it, we must reach beyond our fearful and tense political surroundings to the God who loves us all, the One who enables and asks us to extend this love to others.

CHAPTER TWO

Moral Ambiguity

Bringing faith into politics necessitates bringing in doubt as well. It is certainly more convenient when faith enters politics with only absolute assertions and stark positions, that is to say dogmatically. When this happens, faith serves the political purposes of those advancing particular legislation or campaigning on a certain set of issues. It is akin to the role that ethics sometimes plays in professional contexts. The role of the hired ethicist is not to highlight the gray areas (unless they indicate loopholes perhaps), but rather to provide justification for policy and behavior. In both of these situations, faith and ethics are used instrumentally to serve the interests of those who employ them. To my mind, something is very wrong when faith and ethics enter into a context without somehow stirring it up. At minimum, keeping things neat and clean suggests some form of manipulation to ensure that faith and ethics buttress existing policies or structures rather than challenge them. So, among other things, the elements of doubt and the residue of moral ambiguity are sequestered.

Refusing to play politics with our faith requires the release and inclusion of doubt and ambiguity. I believe that doubt is constitutive of faith, meaning that without doubt, faith is not faith. In other words, faith and doubt are not two distinct things, but inextricably connected such that faith without some element of doubt is inauthentic. When authentic faith enters politics, it complicates things.

This chapter examines the complicating effect of faith by using language of moral ambiguity. Moral ambiguity is a feeling of tension, fragmentation, or uncertainty that persists as one wrestles with an ethical question and even after one has reached a conclusion or made a decision. It is the residue that remains in the form of lingering questions, grief, and doubt. I argue that moral ambiguity cannot and should not be avoided. It cannot be avoided because our ethical reflection is informed by multiple sources of information, because we have competing commitments, and because our positions cause pain to other people and usually involve a "mournful act."[1]

Moral ambiguity *should* not be avoided because the gray areas around even our most certain positions create space for identifying shared concerns, expressing and responding to vulnerability, and nurturing the possibility of reconciliation. Like *agape*, moral ambiguity makes relationship possible. By attending to moral ambiguity, faith may not serve the narrow interests of a legislative or political campaign, but it can contribute to the transformation of antagonistic spaces and divided communities.

Defending Moral Ambiguity

Just as many Christians would dispute my affirmation of doubt as an essential element of faith, many ethicists would dispute my conviction that moral ambiguity is unavoidable. Moral philosophers have frequently argued that ambiguity is symptomatic of an incomplete process of rational deliberation (or even, in more sour moments, as a mark of moral immaturity). And many sharp minds have worked to develop mechanisms to deliberate even the most delicate question without leaving residue. Christian theologian and ethicist James Gustafson explains it this way:

> A great deal of moral philosophy is dedicated to developing basic principles and their application in such a way that most, if not all, conflicts can be resolved rationally. For some moral philosophers there are not genuine moral dilemmas; fully good reasons can be given for every particular choice. There is, in such views, never an occasion for remorse when the well-reasoned choice is made.[2]

In order to secure such clarity, ethicists use a set of general theories or formulae. Does x benefit the least advantaged? Does x secure the greatest good for the greatest number? Is x something that you would will universal? Was action x undertaken with a good intention? Does the positive effect of x outweigh its negative consequences? And yet, for many of us, such moral calculation does not neutralize ambiguity.

In 1999, an American pilot flying a NATO plane at 15,000 feet bombed trucks carrying ethnic Albanian refugees in southern Kosovo. In an unusual response, NATO officials released a copy of the interview with the pilot the following day. The pilot explains that he had seen a convoy of refugees and a "series of villages that had been set on fire, entire villages set on fire." He concludes that Serb forces were "methodically working themselves from the north to the south through villages, setting them ablaze and forcing all the Kosovo Albanians out of their villages." He then sees "another house that has just been ablaze" and "the three-vehicle convoy moving southeast . . . from the freshest-burning house." For twenty-five minutes, the pilot takes "several passes over these vehicles to insure they are in fact military vehicles," until he reaches the conclusion "that these are the people responsible for burning down the

villages that I've seen so far. I go in, put my system on the lead vehi-
cle and execute a laser-guided bomb attack on that vehicle." Because the plane is low on fuel, the pilot leaves and reports the situation to another pilot, who returns to the scene and "proceeds to execute a laser attack on those vehicles." Seventy civilians are killed.[3]

In his remarks about the incident, President Clinton acknowl-
edged it as "regrettable." He continued, "It is also inevitable in a conflict of this kind, with planes traveling at high speeds, doing the best to fulfill their mission. And if the requirement is that nothing like this can ever happen, then we're saying it's O.K. with us if Mr. Milosevic displaces over a million Kosovars, kills and rapes thousands upon thousands of them."[4] President Clinton invoked several principles of just war theory here. By referencing the violence per-
petrated by Milosevic, he argued for the just cause motivating this military response, namely the protection of innocents. He justified the deaths in the convoy by reference to the larger mission of the war, thus utilizing the principle of proportionality, which states that an action is justified if the good intended outweighs the evil done. In language from the United States Catholic Bishops in 1983, this principle of proportionality "means that the damage to be inflicted and the costs incurred by war must be proportionate to the good expected by taking up arms."[5]

Others commenting on this incident informally and those adjudging the pilot's actions formally invoked the principle of double effect, according to which the pilot was not culpable for the unintended outcome, the death of civilians. The principle of dou-
ble effect has ancient roots in the tradition of western moral thought, dating back at least to Aristotle in the fourth century B.C.E. In his lectures, Aristotle distinguished between voluntary actions for which one is culpable and involuntary actions for which

one may be pardoned. In his discussion of involuntary actions, he includes circumstances in which one's act issues in an unintended consequence.[6] In the language of just war theory, civilians must not be the intended target of direct attack, but the unintended consequences of a soldier's actions may be tolerated. As Michael Walzer points out, this ancient and complex principle is truly a relatively common and familiar way of thinking about the unintended consequences of one's actions. We regularly make distinctions between intention and effect and determine to judge a person's behavior based on the former and not the latter. In the context of just war thinking, "Double effect is a way of reconciling the absolute prohibition against attacking noncombatants with the legitimate conduct of military activity."[7] More generally, it is a way to reconcile good intentions with unintended and unanticipated outcomes. And yet, it is a mistake to believe that such "reconciliation" voids moral ambiguity. Even Aristotle argued that the person who commits such an unintended action and, upon realizing the outcome, has no remorse about it is in a different category than the person who "regrets what he [or she] has done."[8]

Drawing on this line of thinking (that is, applying these general principles to this particular situation), one can reach the conclusion that the NATO pilot should not be condemned morally or militarily for the death of the seventy refugees. And I think that one could also respond this way out of care for the pilot personally: "You did the best you could to determine that it was a military vehicle. Given your mission and the information you had, you took the right action." One could also affirm President Clinton's response, following just war logic, that there is a greater good to be accomplished and it outweighs the evil done. However, even if we reach these moral conclusions, it is impossible to sterilize this act, to cleanse it of the guilt, grief, and rage surrounding it.

Because the pilot remained anonymous, there is no photo of him to accompany the transcript of the interview. There are, however, several pictures of the victims. One captures dead bodies next to destroyed vehicles.[9] In another one, a woman grips a man who is lying on the ground, holding his head, and crying.[10] Still another photo bears the caption, "Distraught after her ordeal." Here, a woman gazes down with a grief-stricken look and one hand on the scarf that covers her forehead.[11] Neither the dispassionate defense of the pilot nor President Clinton's passionate appeal to the costs of a just war can settle the emotions stirred up by these photos.

One response to these persistent emotions is to separate them from the process of rational deliberation. These emotions might linger, but they are not a part of ethical deliberation. Thus, they cannot inform our assessment or prompt us to rethink our conclusions. They may be present, but ethical deliberation must remain immune from their influence. I disagree with this position because I understand emotion to be not only an unavoidable aspect of human experience, but also an indicator of meaning and value, and a source of knowledge for us. I am certainly not alone in arguing for the moral value of emotion, although the dominant view in the western moral tradition has been that emotions are "unreliable, animal, seductive."[12]

There is also a trajectory of thought, surfacing periodically in the history of the western moral tradition, that emotions are necessary components of practical reasoning.[13] In its contemporary expression, the argument for emotions includes criticism of the myth of objectivity. We are all embodied persons who cannot interpret, assess, and respond to the world apart from our experience of it. Emotion is one way we interact with the world. We may suppress emotions or claim to otherwise separate them from a process of moral reasoning. But, as philosopher and ethicist Allison Jaggar argues, we cannot act or reason as though such "subterranean emotions do not exert a continuing influence on people's articulated values and observations, thoughts and actions."[14]

Not only is emotion an unavoidable presence in our lives and in the process of responding to the world, it is also desirable because it has a cognitive element and is tied to belief and value. The exact nature of the relationship between belief, value, and emotion is disputed, but for our purposes it is sufficient to acknowledge an unavoidable interaction here. Allison Jaggar argues that "values presuppose emotions" and "emotions presuppose values." "If we had no emotional response to the world, it is inconceivable that we should ever come to value one state of affairs more highly than another."[15] For philosopher Martha Nussbaum, the difference between a more animalistic impulse and an ethical emotion is that the latter has belief as its "necessary basis and 'ground.'"[16] Emotions are "intimately related to beliefs or judgments about the world in such a way that the removal of the relevant belief will remove not only the reason for the emotion but also the emotion itself."[17] That sense of ambiguity—the residue, the needling question—is speaking to us about what we value and encouraging us to keep working toward a response that incorporates this value somehow.

This is not to say, however, that emotions are "self-certifying sources of ethical truth," as Martha Nussbaum points out.[18] They can be unreliable (like beliefs and principles can also be), and they can change. But it is neither possible nor desirable to completely separate emotions from the process of moral reflection. We need mechanisms and practices for utilizing emotions constructively and carefully in the process of moral reflection. There are two helpful, if slightly contradictory, steps one might take. The first is to argue along with Nussbaum and Jaggar that emotion is indeed part of a process of moral deliberation, that it is a source of knowledge and an indicator of value. Thus, we broaden our definition of deliberation to incorporate emotions like complicity, care, and altruism into our rational process, arguing against a bifurcation between reason and emotion.

The second option is to accept a narrower understanding of deliberation and opt for a broader concept of discernment. Ethicist Margaret Farley describes the difference this way.

> The distinction is a readily recognized one between deliberation primarily as a rational process (which may include, for example, clarifying empirical data, weighing reasons, calculating consequences, determining priorities in the application of ethical principles) and discernment as a more complex (imaginative, affective, perhaps aesthetic and even religious) process of searching, illuminating, sifting, recognizing, comprehending, and judging options for moral action against and within a wide horizon of relevant factors.[19]

Language of moral discernment opens the door for attention to affective elements, experiences of tension, grief, doubt, and fragmentation. In the following pages, I argue that attention to these elements can deepen and strengthen our moral reflection. Moreover, I argue that moral ambiguity has a positive, constructive role to play in the public sphere. It may be politically ineffective in a narrow sense. In our political culture, admitting a sense of moral ambiguity translates into being wishy-washy or evasive. Expressions of moral ambiguity do not fit neatly into a sound bite or on a bumper sticker. However, moral ambiguity is an unavoidable companion to the ethically complex issues we face and to a rigorous process of moral reflection. Moreover, feelings of moral ambiguity identify the gray areas where we might find agreement with others. The site of moral ambiguity, the penumbra, is the borderland where people might identify shared concerns, common struggles, and some point of connection to one another. In short, I argue that moral ambiguity, when constructively used, can be politically effective in a deep way: it makes reconciliation possible.

The following pages make the case that moral ambiguity is an unavoidable element in moral thinking for a number of reasons, beginning with the multiple sources of information that inform us. After making the case that moral ambiguity is always with us, I then respond to concerns that it encourages stalling or even fosters paralysis. The chapter ends with practices for working constructively with moral ambiguity.

Ethical and Theological Explanations for Moral Ambiguity

Multiple Sources

Our interpretation of and response to an ethical question are informed by a variety of sources, which Christian ethicists usually categorize under four headings: scripture, tradition, reason, and experience. Methodists may recognize these as the elements of the Wesleyan Quadrilateral, but the four categories are not unique to Wesleyan ethics. It is important to note the plurality within each of these four, even before we think about working with them in tandem.

When we cite Scripture as the basis for our position, we are rarely (if ever) thinking of the Bible in its entirety. Rather, we draw from a canon within the canon. Although this charge raises hackles, it is important to admit that we *all* practice selective use of Scripture. And even when we are more exact about the places in Scripture that inform us, we draw on these passages in a variety of different ways without usually thinking about the difference that our methods make to our deliberation. In sum, the exact content of Scripture and our particular approach to it affect the conclusions we reach. Thus, the outcome of biblically based moral reasoning rests on a variety of contingencies, and responsible Christian ethics requires that we be cognizant of and honest about them. Again, ethics should complicate the context in which it is employed.

One of the most helpful discussions of the role of Scripture in moral discernment comes from James Gustafson, widely recognized for clarifying this discussion of moral sources generally.[20] Gustafson identifies four approaches to the use of Scripture in ethics: law, ideal, analogy, and reflective discourse. For each approach, he raises questions. For example, when one approaches the Scripture as law, we immediately ask which law is being referenced. Is the reference to the Decalogue? To the "new law in Christ"? We also have questions of application. Do we apply the law, for example, Thou Shalt Not Kill, in every situation? As discussed in chapter 1,[21] questions persist when one approaches Scripture as describing/commending ideal human behavior. If we take, for example, the hard sayings to indicate ideal human behavior, then are we to assume that an ideal can be realized? Do we work toward it, hoping for an approximation? Or is the expectation that we will strive toward it, knowing that compromise with the world is required for responsible living?

Analogy is the third approach to Scripture that Gustafson identifies. After September 11, I invited several guests to my class for an informal panel of perspectives on pacifism and just war. During the discussion, one student drew the following analogy: "It's like the U.S. is David; and we have to fight against the terrorists who are Goliath." My colleague in Biblical Studies very calmly replied, "OK, but what if we are Goliath?" Her point was excellent on several levels. First, she succinctly captured the perspective shared by many in the world that the United States is an imperial power threatening the autonomy of cultures and nations. Second, she demonstrated both the power and the malleability of analogy. In Gustafson's language, she illustrated the problem of control. What drives the analogy? What prompts you to choose a particular narrative to interact with? What prompts you to assign the roles as you do? "If present events are in control, then one first responds to these events and then on the basis of that response seeks biblical events that are similar to the present ones. The predisposition is to seek those events which will confirm one's present judgments."[22] In many ways, analogy is a very natural move because it involves interacting and identifying with a story. It is also a move to make transparently and greet suspiciously. We need to be honest about the reasons we gravitate toward a particular story and identify with a particular character. And, we need to respond to other people's analogies with questions about control rather than accepting each analogy as crafted.

The fourth approach, which Gustafson titles "reflective discourse," acknowledges the variety of "moral values, moral norms and principles" present in Scripture, as well as, their different forms of expression (mandate, story, etc.) and the "particular historical contexts" to which they were originally directed. Given the variance within the texts and the contextual chasm between their time and our own, reflective discourse utilizes Scripture as one source among many. Moreover, it does not use only one theme, one ideal, or one law and apply it to an ethical question in a straightforward way. Rather, one engages a process "of reflective discourse about present events *in light of* appeals to this variety of material as well as to other principles and experiences. Scripture is one of the informing sources for moral judgments, but it is not sufficient in itself to make any particular judgment authoritative."[23]

Gustafson rightly describes this approach as the "loosest" of the four and notes that it yields less biblically authoritative conclusions. In the third chapter, we will wrestle with this method more directly because it represents the approach of many (like myself) who are deeply informed by the tradition of liberal theology and who believe that the variety within and the contexts of the texts must be acknowledged, even though they weaken the Bible's authority as a "moral witness."[24]

So far, we have only considered one informing source, namely Scripture, and already we see considerable variety in terms of content and approach. Awareness of the contingency of Christian ethics only grows as we consider other informing sources, such as tradition. Here too, we find considerable variety among Protestants and between Protestants and Catholics. Some Protestants, for example, view tradition as too unreliable and contaminated by human fallibility to be a moral resource. Therefore, they claim to hold to Scripture alone, *sola scriptura*. Other Protestants like Stanley Hauerwas suggest that Scripture does not have moral authority apart from tradition. It is the community formed by the texts that imbue them with authority. So, one cannot rely on—or even turn to—Scripture without turning to the community of faith that gives the narratives their meaning and authority.[25] Most Roman Catholics hold that the Bible is silent on important issues and in need of interpretation. The writings of the church, such as papal encyclicals, cooperate with Scripture to form sacred tradition.

Others, and I place myself here, approach tradition as a record of Christians' interaction with the world. In this record, I do not see something "basically continuous and conservative," but rather a collection of "ongoing conversations or arguments subject to dramatic reversal and, at times, revolutionary innovation."[26] In tradition, therefore, one finds not so much a resource for "the truth," as a record of people grappling with multiple truths and their meaning in changing times. However, this does not mean that "anything goes." The record includes such wrestling because people are trying to maintain a connection between the faith and a changing world, to interact with the world in a way that one might also describe as Christian. Thus, there is interplay between changing context and the core commitments of the faith, and the interplay includes efforts to determine what those core commitments are. Douglas Ottati describes interacting with this record as "standing in a living tradition." "To stand in a living tradition, then, is to participate in a dynamic process of interpretation—one that moves between received heritage and the realities and challenges of the present world in order to express a continuing and vital orientation or identity."[27]

The third category, reason, includes information from philosophy and the sciences. This category seems to attract the most attention as a site of conflict. Certainly, the relationship between the contents of this category and that of others is under constant debate. However, interaction between faith and reason has a long history and now assumes many different forms. Thomas Aquinas is widely recognized for his systematic integration of Greek philosophy and Christian theology. The natural law tradition has had a prominent position in Roman Catholic thought and practice since the Middle Ages. Today, in the field of Christian ethics, it is a foundational assumption that one cannot address the issues of our day without understanding them in their own terms. Thus, depending on the issue itself, one must become conversant with science, politics, economics, or psychology.

For example, consider James Gustafson's observations about the role that empirical sciences play in ethical thinking. First, he notes that "psychological, sociological, and anthropological studies have had a very significant impact in recent decades on the *understanding of persons*."[28] We rely on these social sciences to teach us about human behavior and development. Gustafson also observes that we rely on sciences "to get a more precise and complete *understanding of the circumstances* in which a moral problem occurs, and thus in defining both the causes and options for action"[29] and "to assist [us] in *predicting the consequences of certain choices*."[30] These observations hold true for the social and "hard" sciences. We need the sciences to understand the process of global warming and options for recourse, the mechanics of poverty and the requirements for alleviating it, and the contexts of conflict and possibilities for reconciliation. And we rely on the sciences to adjudicate between options so that we have a greater likelihood of accomplishing our goal.

Gustafson's fourth observation is a more complex one because it acknowledges a problematic use of the social sciences "in the *development of moral norms*."[31] For good and ill, we do rely on the sciences not only to describe our situation and range of choices, but also to determine what ought to be done. With this observation, Gustafson supports the point that the sciences should be one informing source among others in moral deliberation.

The fourth category of moral source is experience. Like the other three categories, this one is also a place of plurality and debate. I take as my starting point Margaret Farley's definition of experience.

> What I shall mean by "experience" in this essay is the actual living of events and relationships, along with the sensations, feelings, images, emotions, insights, and understandings that are part of this lived reality. Experience in this sense is a given, something providing data to be interpreted; but it is also something that is already interpreted, its content shaped by previous understandings in a context of multiple influences. Moreover, experience, as I shall address it, can belong both to the self and to others; it can

be both personal and social. Experience is private, individual, unique to the one who experiences; but there are shared experiences, communicated as well as formed within communities and societies. Experience in each of these senses—given but not primitive, immediate but not innocent of interpretation, personal but not isolated, unique but not without a social matrix—plays an important role in moral discernment. It is a source of moral insight, a factor in moral judgment, a test of the rightness, goodness, and wisdom of a moral decision.[32]

I also agree with Farley's argument that

> experience is never just one source among many. It is always an important part of the context of each of the other sources, and it is always a key factor in the interpretation of the others. Scripture, for example, is the record of some persons' experience of God; tradition represents a community's experience through time; humanistic and even scientific studies are shaped by the experience of those who engage in them. Past experience, therefore, provides content for all of the sources, and present experience provides a necessary and inescapable vantage point for interpreting them.[33]

Experience is debated as a moral source, primarily because it seems to open the door to relativism. If experience is an authority and a criterion for testing truth and determining what is right and good, then doesn't anything go? I understand this concern and will address elements of it in the following paragraphs, but I also think that it is rooted in the false assumption that we can in fact set experience aside and engage a moral question without recourse to it. Experience—"the contemporary actual living of events and relationships"[34]—is the very stuff of our reflection. And past experiences inevitably inform our response.

The question is therefore not whether to use experience, but how to use it. My recommendation is that we reflect on our experience transparently and critically, meaning that we are clear to ourselves and others about the way our place in the world affects the way we respond to an event. We are clear with ourselves and others about our inclinations and biases, and we invite others to be open about theirs as well. Along these lines, then, we use experience dialogically, not dogmatically. When we deny the role of experience, then we speak about *our* interaction with the world as though it were the *only* interaction with the world. What is truthfully my partial and slanted perspective on things masquerades as an objective assessment, as truth.

Finally, we draw on experience communally as well as individually. I do not experience things alone; there are others who have had similar experiences. There is a shared experience that can inform me, check my assumptions and inclinations, and hold me accountable to what really happened.

This is not to say that experience is "self-certifying truth."[35] On this point, I agree with Margaret Farley, who writes, "I do not . . . adopt a fundamentalist view of the authority of experience. I am therefore not committed to agreeing with every conclusion that is drawn from experience."[36] Experience must be one informing source, among others. Because experience has been the most devalued source of the quadrilateral, those of us who defend it do so in a particularly vigorous way. However, to insist that experience is authoritative is not to say that "only experience is authoritative or that it is ever sufficient for Christian moral discernment."[37] It is one legitimate source of knowledge among many.

Scripture, tradition, reason, and experience each contain plurality and internal contradiction, and their interaction is one reason for the persistence of moral ambiguity. However, that this does not mean that approaches that draw on multiple sources are bad. Rather, I think that our processes of moral discernment *should* draw on multiple sources, and that moral ambiguity is part of this necessary interaction. What we strive for is some kind of consonance between these informing sources so that we have enough agreement to take a step. However, it is rare that the guidance from these different directions harmonizes completely. We might also determine to weigh one source more heavily than the others in a given situation. However, doing so does not nullify the other sources completely or make us magically unaware of the different conclusions to which they direct us. We must not only consult these multiple sources of insight in a process of moral discernment, but also acknowledge the residue that remains as we reach our best moral conclusion.

Competing Commitments

A second explanation for moral ambiguity is that we often hold commitments that are in tension with one another. The following example of tension between pacifist and feminist commitments also illustrates the way in which ambiguity is exacerbated by the necessary presence of multiple informing sources.

In the early 1990s, I attended the University of Notre Dame for a master's degree from the Kroc Institute for International Peace Studies. Although the master's students came from a variety of geographical, ethnic, and religious backgrounds, we often took courses with Roman Catholic students in the undergraduate peace studies program. One such course was on nonviolent social change with David Cortright, previously the director of SANE/FREEZE. On the day we were to discuss use of the media, I brought to class a media packet from a rally some of the master's students had just attended in Washington D.C. It was a march for reproductive freedom and abortion rights organized by the National Organization for Women. I marvel now at my naiveté, but I honestly shared the packet only as an example related to the class subject for the day. The embarrassing fact is that I did not think about the affront this packet represented to the Roman Catholic pro-life students in the class. We sat in a large circle, listening to David while the packet floated around the room. Then, quietly but deliberately, a fellow student received the packet, walked to an open window, and threw it out of the second-floor classroom.

A passionate and awkward exchange followed, in which I clarified my intention and the student explained the affront. I had certainly experienced conflict in a classroom before, but I had never felt it so viscerally. That day frequently comes back to me as the first time I began thinking about my dual commitment to pacifism and to a woman's right to bodily integrity (control of her body). I continue to hold both of these commitments and to struggle with the tensions between them.

As a pacifist, I see that of God in every person and believe that we destroy something sacred whenever we take a human life. However, I am persuaded by scientific argument that life begins at the point of viability. When the fetus can live independently of its mother, then it has personhood. Until that point, the embryo is a part of the woman's body, and the life we care for is hers. Reflecting on my own experiences of pregnancy, I had the feeling that something sacred was in process and that I was responsible for someone else long before the point of viability outside the womb. But I am also aware that the desire for children and the context of a loving marriage shaped my feelings about pregnancy. I cannot imagine feeling the same way about a pregnancy that was forced upon me; nor would I ever dream of imposing such feelings on a woman whose pregnancy is involuntary. This suggests that the feeling of sacredness that I had during my pregnancy stemmed not from a belief in the inherent value of an embryo beginning at conception, but rather from the larger context surrounding my own pregnancies. I cannot, therefore, impose such feelings on other women whose circumstances differ from my own. Nor can I, consequently, impose the convictions that accompany the feeling. That is, I cannot extend my pacifist commitment to the embryo in another woman's womb based on my own experience of sacredness. The resistance to imposition is further sustained by a commitment to bodily integrity, the principle that a person must have control over her own body. And so, I ultimately affirm a woman's right to reproductive freedom. I do so recognizing the many mournful elements of abortion, including the context of the pregnancy, the loss of a potential life, and the tragedy of a world with unwanted children.

I am aware that the preceding paragraphs contain tenuous lines of argument, making my dual commitment vulnerable to attack from all sides. The point is not to defend this dual commitment, but to risk articulating it in an honest way, a practice that I will reference in the latter section of this chapter. To varying degrees, competing commitments complicate our decisions every day. A vegetarian deliberates whether to eat meat so as not to offend her host. Parents wrestle with their commitment to providing their child with the best possible education and their commitment to support the public school system. Pastors struggle with their prophetic and pastoral roles, wanting to preach boldly and minister to a diverse congregation. Those working in cross-cultural settings respect cultural autonomy and value certain universal human rights. Caregivers grapple with tensions between their own convictions concerning treatment and their commitment to patient autonomy. And every day, in countless settings, people juggle a sense of fairness with a desire to respond to the particular needs of an individual.

This last example in particular highlights the point that "competing commitments" does not only mean incompatibility between moral principles.[38] It also means that we often wrestle with tension between general principles to which we are fully committed and the particular needs of individuals that such principles either overlook or fail to address completely. This form of moral ambiguity is exacerbated by ethical approaches that attend to particulars, context, and narrative. Again, I am not arguing that the method is the problem. Like multiple informing sources, this ethical method is good *and* contributes to ambiguity.

For example, when a student approaches me with a legitimate request for extending the deadline for an assignment, I wrestle with two commitments: (1) to meet the individual needs of the student in front of me and (2) to be fair to the other students in the class, many of whom have similar demands and are submitting the work on time. Carol Gilligan describes these commitments as reflecting two moral orientations, care and justice. In the care orientation, one attends to the particular needs of individual people. We also tend to be more aware of the larger narrative surrounding the exact question or moment. And we see the moral act in terms of responding to needs and maintaining relationships. In the justice orientation, we work with an eye toward fairness, aiming toward consistent treatment, conforming our response to rules that transcend the particular moment and people involved. Gilligan suggests that we can access both of these orientations, but each one dominates at different times. Her analogy is an ink blot test; one minute you see two faces; the next minute you see the hourglass.[39]

One can sense moral ambiguity within either the care or the justice orientation, but moral ambiguity increases with movement back and forth between them, a movement that is necessary. While the promised tidiness of general principles and the substantive value of fairness are attractive, we must consider the particulars and think about the larger narrative surrounding the ethical question. We must aim for justice and fairness in decision-making, and we must reflect on the particular needs of the concrete persons affected by the decision. Is x best for her? Is x what he needs? How did the student get into this situation exactly?[40] If we then zoom out from this individual student, we might be prompted to think about the larger structural issues that contributed to the student's inability to complete the assignment on time, such as the demands of the curriculum for second career or commuter students.

Again, the problem is not a method of ethical reasoning that attends to people and relationships as well as to more general principles. The "problem" is that we are relational beings trying to live out commitments that impact the lives of others. We need to practice forms of ethics that attend to those relationships and wrestle with the various forms of ambiguity that result as we care for one another.

Awareness of Pain My Decision Causes Another

Attention to relationships suggests another cause of moral ambiguity, namely an awareness of the pain that a decision or position causes another person. If I grant the extension, I may cause pain to a student who was in a similar situation and yet got his work in on time. If I do not grant the extension, I cause pain to the student who requested it. Sometimes, the pain we cause is deeper than the kind of grudge or resentment that clings to these classroom examples. For example, I am aware that my conviction that the Iraq war is immoral and unjust may cause deep pain to and prompt understandable anger from the parent of a soldier who dies there.

Let me offer another example of this provided by Mary June Nestler, when she was my faculty colleague and Dean of the Episcopal Theological School at Claremont. In August 2003, Mary

June attended the annual General Convention of the Episcopal Church. She was there for the intense debate over Gene Robinson's episcopacy and the vote that confirmed him as the first openly gay bishop. When we gathered for our annual faculty retreat a few weeks later, Mary June shared this experience, and her account has stayed with me. She told us that she and others who fully supported Bishop Robinson's confirmation received this victory soberly. What struck me about Mary June's account, however, was that they received this victory soberly *not* because this confirmation would fuel the division rather than quell it. (After all, a vote against Bishop Robinson's confirmation would have had the same effect.) Rather, they received this victory soberly out of love and concern for those whose position was defeated. Mary June's example is helpful to us because it demonstrates that some feelings of moral ambiguity are related not to the conviction per se, but to the implications of that conviction for other people. I can feel certain about my position and still feel empathy toward those who think differently.

What prompts (or sustains) this sense of feeling for someone with whom we disagree? It is hard to say exactly or entirely, but one cause is that our disagreement (deep and antagonistic as it might be) occurs in the context of a much larger narrative. And in that larger narrative, our positions are less absolute, and we are connected to one another in various ways. In the context of that broader narrative, I am more aware of the mournful element of every position. Beyond the clarity of my own position on the war, I see its affront to veterans who have given themselves to an effort that I deem immoral. Beyond the clarity that the United States presence in Iraq exacerbates the violence, I see the tragedy of violence that will continue after we leave. A moral question is never isolated. It is always part of a larger narrative. Circumstances unfold that give rise to the question; conditions develop after a decision is carried out. In our reflection on the preceding circumstances, we will often find reason for self-implication. As we live through the subsequent events, we will often find reason to doubt the decision made. Again, I emphasize that this residue persists even if we were certain about our decision. As Gustafson argues so persuasively, even the most thoroughly deliberated and discerned position can issue in a "'mournful' act." "The tragic character of many actions resides precisely in the fact that the legitimate pursuit of legitimate ends, or action in accordance with reasonable moral principles, entails severe losses to others—not only persons but other living things—and even sometimes diminishes the possibilities for development of future life and future generations of human beings."[41]

Awareness of this larger narrative also means that we see overlapping identities and concerns aside from the issue that divides us. My identity extends beyond being anti-war and pro-gay. Those are commitments that I hold, and they place me on a certain side in each debate. But I am also a mother, and I have friends who have served in Iraq, and these pieces of my identity help me to identify with the fierce commitments of the soldier's mother. There is a sense (which we cannot always access in the heat of a conflict) that we remain in relationship with people even though issues divide us. Sometimes that relationship is more tangible: we share a denomination or a community organization. Other times the relationship is more vague. But either way, we remain accountable to those people with whom we disagree, and I think we have a moral duty to cultivate empathy toward them when it does not come naturally.

This point is closely related to the *agape* discussion in the previous chapter. Walter Wink makes this connection plain in *The Powers that Be* (1999). He also provides theological support for the moral call to empathy and a sense of relatedness.

> Our solidarity with our enemies lies not just in our common parentage under God, but also our common evil. God "is kind to the ungrateful and the wicked." We too, like them, betray what we know in our hearts God desires for the world. We would like to identify ourselves as just and good, but we are a mix of just and unjust, good and evil. . . . As we begin to acknowledge our own inner shadow, we become more tolerant of the shadow in others. As we begin to love the enemy within, we develop the compassion we need to love the enemy without.[42]

The language of enemy sounds abrupt on the heels of the previous examples, but the point does indeed apply. That is, we attend to the pain our decision causes another, in part, because our own shortcomings and painful experiences prevent self-righteous insensitivity. Like my students, I have overcommitted and missed deadlines, and some people have shown me mercy. Like the mother of the soldier, I have remained loyal to someone whose work involved something I would not otherwise condone. Like Mary June's counterparts, I have certainly been on the losing side of issues for which I was passionate. But even more than this: I have made poor decisions, been insensitive to others, behaved selfishly, and avoided a necessary conflict. In short, I have done things to alienate myself from God and others.

This kind of awareness complicates advocacy and activism in the public square. In the words of Philip Wogaman, "in no simple way can political contests be reduced to a struggle of the forces of righteousness against the forces of evil."[43] As with each explanation of moral ambiguity discussed in this chapter, awareness of the pain my position causes another is not a bad thing. Rather, such an empathetic capacity is worth defending even if it complicates political advocacy in the short run. The complicating nature of moral ambiguity is one of several concerns addressed in the following section.

Problems with Moral Ambiguity

Really, There Is No Ambiguity about Peace, Poverty, and Planet Earth

One immediate response to the material of this chapter is a flat rejection of its central thesis: there really is no ambiguity about the central, substantive issues now identified by progressive Christian leaders: peace, poverty, and planet earth. At the level of goals, I quite agree. I have no ambivalence about the goals of peace, ending poverty, and caring for the earth. But moral ambiguity pervades the details in several ways, and I will offer examples shortly. First, it is worth noting the ambiguity that surrounds the prioritizing of this agenda.

One of the criticisms of the moral values language used during the 2004 presidential campaign was its narrow focus on homosexuality and abortion. In response, progressive Christians repeatedly argued that peace, social justice, and environmental care are also moral values. And in recent years, "peace, poverty, and planet earth" have gained momentum as the progressive Christian agenda.[44] The focus on these three values is also a strategic move on the part of leaders in the progressive Christian movement who see their faith community divided over homosexuality and abortion. So, for example, Bob Edgar (liberal, pro-choice, and supportive of gay marriage) and Jim Wallis (progressive evangelical, pro-life, and supportive of civil unions but not gay marriage) both argue that Christians "remember the vast common ground—those two thousand references to poverty and peace—that unites us."[45] I agree with a broader definition of morality, and I also agree with the accompanying rationale that these concerns (particularly war and poverty) receive significantly more biblical attention than abortion and homosexuality. However, the danger has been to suggest that abortion and homosexuality are somehow negotiable, as we collaborate on the other goals. So, we have a situation in which the most prominent spokespeople for progressive Christianity (and I am thinking beyond Edgar and Wallis here) are heterosexual men who are tabling restriction to women's freedom and the denigration of homosexual love in order to forge alliances for peace, poverty, and planet earth. Even those who fully agree with the biblical warrant and the strategic motivation for prioritizing the agenda this way surely experience concern for the people rendered negotiable. The agenda itself is clouded with moral ambiguity.

Ambiguity also persists as we think about these general goals in more particular ways. I have given multiple examples in this chapter of moral ambiguity related to the goal of peace. And I have not yet mentioned the most difficult question confronting pacifists, namely military intervention to stop genocide. There is simply no way to grapple with the goal of peace in such a violent world without experiencing "fierce ambivalence."[46]

I have no ambivalence over the goal of ending poverty, but public policy discussions regularly make a distinction between deserving and undeserving poor that makes me uneasy. In his book addressing this issue, sociologist Michael Katz explained the problem this way:

> The undeserving poor have a very old history. They represent the enduring attempt to classify poor people by merit. This impulse to classify has persisted for centuries partly for reasons of policy. Resources are finite. Neither the state nor private charity can distribute them in unlimited quantities to all who might claim need. . . . However, scarce resources have been only one reason for classifying poor people. For in poverty discourse, moral assessments have nearly always overlain pragmatic distinctions. The issue becomes not only who can fend for themselves without aid, but

more important, whose behavior and character entitle them to the resources of others.[47]

In addition to ambivalence over such classifications and moral assessments of desert, another source of moral ambiguity related to issues of poverty is awareness of the ways in which we benefit from the oppression of others. There is no clear line between oppressor and oppressed here. Rather, many of us hold "multiple social locations," which give us varying amounts of power. Mary Hobgood addresses her recent book, *Dismantling Privilege*, to "those who enjoy relatively more amounts of social privilege than they suffer subordination."[48] While the thrust of her book is to call us to acknowledge our "unearned privilege" and learn to share power, she does acknowledge the presence of moral ambiguity. She writes:

> The moral responsibility of most elites is complex and ambiguous. . . . Insofar as we occupy multiple social locations, the lack of power and freedom we experience from our membership in subordinate groups may blind us to the power we have as members of dominant groups. Our moral situation is complex. We must acknowledge both our pain and our privilege, both how we are constrained and where we have power, if we are to attain responsible moral agency.[49]

Hobgood's work is another helpful example because there is nothing vague or evasive in her call to moral accountability. She is forthright and clear about her position that unshared power is the root of injustice, and she does effectively call us to task. But her work maintains awareness of the complexity of social locations and the tangle of race, gender, and class that situate us differently and in multiple ways.

I have no ambivalence over the general commitment to planetary health and sustainability. But when we think in more detail about the needs of the planet, ambiguity surfaces. James Gustafson has forcefully articulated this in his work on theocentric ethics where he observes that the health and well-being of the planet may not correspond with the health and well-being of humans.[50] We are participants in a universe that predates us and will outlive us unless we destroy it. It is as difficult to deny this reality as it is to embrace it without ambiguity. Theologian Sallie McFague makes a similar observation about competing interests. In her book, *Life Abundant*, she reflects on the question, "Is reality good?" and offers a qualified response of "yes, but. . . ." One reason for the qualified response is that

> the evolutionary, ecological understanding of reality is so complex in terms of causes, changes, and intents among the billions of animate and inanimate constituents and forces that compose the universe that one has to ask, "good for whom?" What is good for the mosquito is not for the naked arm; the heart transplant that saves my life comes at the cost of another's life; the flood that destroys homes may benefit the crops.[51]

In a recent essay titled, "Ensuring Sustainability," John Cobb alludes to another site of moral ambiguity, namely tension between the short-term needs of the poor and the long term needs of the planet. Now, of course, the poor also need a sustainable planet. Cobb does not draw a sharp distinction here between the needs of the planet as over against the needs of the poor. But he does argue that a Christian commitment to "protect the poor and weak [and] also be in solidarity with them" does not always "entail agreeing with them in their assessments and policy proposals." He continues,

> Those who live from hand to mouth necessarily focus their attention on what is needed so that they can obtain food and shelter for themselves and their families in the immediate future. This short-term orientation can be exploited by the economic and political establishment. It may also be exploited by religious charlatans and the sellers of drugs. Our task as Christians who are not under such immediate economic and psychological pressure is to

view matters in a broader context, both with regard to the social order now and the longer term prospects.[52]

Cobb's point is that this longer-range view is more responsible to the needs of the poor than consenting to short-term practices that temporarily boost an economy while debilitating the country in the long run. We are seeing, for example, the ways in which slash-and-burn agriculture and export economies strip developing nations of natural resources, thus damaging both their ecological and economic health over time. But even certainty about the importance of the long-range view cannot neutralize concern for the immediate needs of the world's poor. Long-range planning for ecological sustainability, though the right thing, still admits a mournful element.

For these examples of moral ambiguity related to poverty and to planet earth, I have purposefully cited Christian theologians and ethicists who are widely recognized as leaders in the movements for economic justice and environmental sustainability. These are not people who are unsure about their positions or hesitant with their arguments. They all call us to task. Still, we find in their writing acknowledgement of moral ambiguity, places where questions linger, where difficulties surface, and a mournful element persists. Such references to moral ambiguity have the positive, constructive effect of preparing us for a difficult and complex task, of calling us to think through the issues in their proper complexity, of wrestling with competing insights and commitments.

Paralysis

The previous examples help to address a second concern, namely that moral ambiguity may be paralyzing. This broken world does demand response and action, and we cannot afford to spend time wringing our hands. There is also a deeper criticism attached to this concern, namely that talk of moral ambiguity is one strategy that those who benefit from the status quo use to maintain it. I understand and agree with these points. Certainly, references to complexity are an easy stalling tactic for those who either benefit from a situation or are not significantly affected by it to motivate genuine concern and redress. So, I agree that some level of suspicion is warranted. However, I am not arguing for a moratorium on action for social change. Rather, I am arguing that moral ambiguity and moral certitude frequently co-exist, such that we can feel some certainty about an issue and still experience unease related to it. The concern about paralysis rests on a false assumption that moral ambiguity and moral certitude are two distinct and mutually exclusive experiences. It is crucial to see that we do not have either moral ambiguity or moral certitude. Rather, both often inhabit us. We have some clarity about a question, and an accompanying gray area. Sister Helen Prejean's account of her relationship with men on death row offers profound examples of this blend of certitude and ambiguity. Speaking of Patrick Sonnier, she writes: "We soon become steady correspondents, and I begin to think of him as a fellow human being, though I can't for a moment forget his crime, nor can I reconcile the easygoing Cajun who writes to me with the brutal murderer of two helpless teenagers."[53]

The first time Prejean visits him in prison, she receives a picture frame that Sonnier made from cigarette wrappers. She reflects, "These hands that made the nice picture frame for me also held a rifle that killed."[54] And yet, alongside this "fierce ambivalence" courses an unshakable certainty: "In sorting out my feelings and beliefs, there is, however, one piece of moral ground of which I am absolutely certain: if I were to be murdered I would not want my murderer executed."[55] And, later, "I still maintain that the state should not kill him. For me, the unnegotiable moral bedrock on which a society must be built is that killing by anyone, under any conditions, cannot be tolerated. And that includes the government."[56]

Among other things, these feelings of ambivalence prompted Sister Helen to brave a relationship with the victims' families. By doing so, she found a way to use the feeling of moral ambiguity constructively, knowing that it would not simply go away. Hers is an important example for us: someone who acts bravely with the strength of her conviction, remains attentive to the accompanying dis-ease, and finally acts in response to the ambivalence itself.

Not Politically Effective

A third concern about attention to moral ambiguity is that it is not politically effective. Especially when one has been the underdog in the public square and is now vigorously working to regain territory and voice, she or he needs to make strong, unequivocal statements to counter the dominant position. Again, there is great truth here. Admitting the places where we wrestle with moral questions assumes a certain amount of power and strength because such admission makes us vulnerable. In a context of intense conflict where one is daily countering absolutist and dogmatic claims that threaten one's core commitments, admitting moral ambiguity actually threatens our cause. In such a context, you must bring your strongest game.

This context of intense conflict where one's arguments are more often subject to disrespectful dismissal than genuine engagement is, truthfully, not unlike the arena in which many ethicists are trained. While in graduate school, I was encouraged to read an essay about "going for the jugular" before delivering my first paper at a national conference. The idea was that I needed to know how to defend myself from criticism and levy devastating rebuttals at my opponent. I never followed the article's instruction, and I now try to foster a different kind of engagement that may be critical without being antagonistic. As a teacher, I work intentionally each semester to establish in my classes a "pounce-free zone." I tell students that this is a space where they will be encouraged to think through moral dilemmas in their complexity without being expected to have a fully formed argument each time they raise their hand. I encourage them to be clear about the places where they feel certain and honest about the places where they struggle. And I instruct them to be respectful toward one another by challenging each other constructively when appropriate and listening empathetically when needed. This pedagogical commitment is one way that I try to change the context that formed me. I do not pretend to think that we can transform the public square as a whole into a pounce-free zone. But I do think that we can establish pounce-free zones among ourselves, as we engage opponents in discussion. This is one of the constructive strategies I will discuss in the final section.

The concern about political effectiveness also warrants qualification. I agree that attention to moral ambiguity is not politically effective in a narrow sense. Moral ambiguity does not fit into a sound bite or on a bumper sticker. It does not win debates or sway public opinion. But attention to and admission of moral ambiguity is politically effective in the deeper sense that I alluded to early in this chapter. When we identify the penumbra, the gray area, around our moral position, we open up a space for dialogue. We may feel like we are opening up a space for the opponent's fatal blow, but we are also taking a risk to make possible genuine, heart-felt dialogue with those who struggle in a similar way even though their sphere of moral certainty stands apart from our own. One standard feature in conflict resolution is to encourage the parties to a conflict to identify the interests underlying their positions.[57] What happens is that disputants find that they have some common interests that they could not see when they were focused on their more narrowly articulated positions. The step of identifying interests is analogous to the admission of moral ambiguity, in my mind. It is a risky move that increases the possibility of understanding in the short term and reconciliation in the future.

Constructive Practices for Using Moral Ambiguity

The overarching thesis of this chapter is that moral ambiguity is an unavoidable companion to moral discernment. This does not mean that we have no sense of moral certainty; nor does it suggest an inability to act with conviction. But it does mean that we continue to experience tension, fragmentation, lingering questions, and grief, even as we pursue those things we believe in. It also means that sometimes we struggle to discern the appropriate response and wrestle with competing commitments or the implications of our position for others. In the situations where we do feel more certain, we need to attend to the residue to avoid dogmatism and narrow-mindedness. In the situations where we feel more ambiguity than certainty, we must identify enough certitude to move forward without denying these feelings of ambivalence. So, the question for the final section of this chapter is how to use moral ambiguity constructively in our ongoing processes of moral discernment and in our actions.

See Action and Reflection as Elements of an Ongoing Process, Rather than Two Distinct Steps

It is a mistake, in my view, to separate moral activity into distinct components of thinking and acting. Yes, we need to do a certain amount of study, analysis, and reflection in order to determine the best course of action or the most fitting response. But it is a mistake to assume that this process of discernment must come to a tidy conclusion before any action can take place, or that once we begin to act, the time for study and analysis is past. My experience has been that careful study and reflection on a moral question at some point yields a certain amount of surety that I envision as a paving stone. I have enough clarity and enough conviction to take a step, write a letter of protest, participate in an action, or offer a statement to a group or a class. But I also find that such actions frequently raise further questions, sending me back for more reflection. So, the first and most basic suggestion for responding constructively to moral ambiguity is to keep in mind the dynamic nature of this process of moral reflection and action. It takes the form of praxis, an ongoing interaction between theory and practical activity, or a cyclical process of movement from reflection to action and back to reflection again.

Identify the Source of Moral Ambiguity as Exactly as Possible

In this dynamic process of reflection-action-reflection, we must aim to identify the source of moral ambiguity as exactly as possible. Frequently, the residue is palpable but hard to pin down. We have a feeling of unease, but cannot quite locate its source. However, the work of moral discernment requires that we do so. We need to work hard to locate the source of ambivalence. Feeling the edge of the paving stone with your foot is a place to start. Or you might remember what it is like to place paper over a penny and rub it with a crayon. The shape of the penny is distinct, with a particularly sharp circle marking its edge. Locating that space, the circumference of your certainty, is part of the task. But then, we need to sort through the penumbra, the gray area. What is at stake in this matter? What are the lingering questions? What data do you feel that you need but do not yet have? Who are the people who come to mind when you let yourself focus on the unease? Are they people who disagree with you? What is the exact nature of that disagreement? Is your unease prompted by a general discomfort with conflict or by a point they make that you cannot satisfactorily rebut? Are the people who come to mind those who are adversely affected by the position you hold? Should their pain prompt you to rethink your position? Or is it the case that they will be affected negatively no matter what happens, and that tragic awareness causes you grief? Do you experience tension between competing commitments? Are there informing sources, which you consider authoritative, not in concert here, prompting you to weigh one more heavily than another?

Once the source has been identified more exactly, another decision point emerges. We have to determine if the source of our ambiguity is sufficient to prompt re-evaluation of our decision or position. If the decision holds, can the moral ambiguity be resolved somehow? If not, does it beg a task that we can identify and pursue? Again, I turn to Sister Helen Prejean's autobiographical reflection for a helpful example of this part of the process. Early in her correspondence with Sonnier, Sister Helen writes of her feelings of guilt. She considers visiting prisoners to be an act of charity consistent with her vocation, and she fervently believes that killing—no matter who does it—is wrong. Yet, she feels guilty. She writes,

> I cannot accept that the state now plans to kill Patrick Sonnier in cold blood. But the thought of the young victims haunts me. Why do I feel guilty when I think of them? Why do I feel as if I have murdered someone myself? In prayer I sort it out. I know that if I had been at the scene when the young people were abducted, I would have done all in my power to save them. I know I feel compassion for their suffering parents and family and

would do anything to ease their pain if I knew how. I also know that nothing can ease their pain. I know I am trying to help people who are desperately poor, and I hope I can prevent some of them from exploding into violence. Here my conscience is clean and light. No heaviness, no guilt. Then it comes to me. The victims are dead and the killer is alive and I am befriending the killer.[58]

These feelings of guilt do not prompt her to re-evaluate her position on the death penalty. She remains firmly against it. But these feelings do propel the very difficult action of engaging the victims' families.

Establish Pounce-free Zones

The understandable impulse when we feel uncertain about something is to seek out those who can reassure us that our position is indeed correct. So, we continue to talk and work with people of like mind, people who can help us dispel these feelings of ambivalence or at least reassure us that we are right, in spite of them. I practice and benefit from this kind of fellowship myself. However, my job affords me the opportunity to engage those who disagree on a regular basis, and such engagement is also tremendously beneficial. As indicated earlier, I believe that exchanges among people who disagree need to have some ground rules in order for moral ambiguity to be acknowledged and constructively utilized.

One such ground rule is the establishment of a "pounce-free zone," a place where individuals can think through complex moral questions together without fear of someone pouncing on them. It is a place where disagreements are explored conversationally rather than debated antagonistically. Participants in these conversations explain their position without fear that others are poised to attack the weak place. And we work to hear some truth within the other's perspective rather than listening for the error. This form of discourse does not aim toward agreement necessarily, but it does remain open to common ground. The purpose of the conversation is understanding rather than conversion. A pounce-free zone is primarily an educational space, a space where we meet to understand others and to clarify our own views and the limitations of them.

One conversation strategy in these zones is described by Carol Lakey Hess, professor of religious education, as "Q&W."[59] Rather than a period of Q&A (question and answer), Lakey Hess invites participants to question and wrestle. Strategies like this establish the appropriate tone for conversation: There are no easy answers here, and we are all struggling. It is important, therefore, to aim for as much even participation in these conversations as possible. Additional strategies can help with this. For example, I often give students an opportunity to reflect on a question individually in writing (if they prefer) before we begin the discussion. This gives the "mullers" time to mull, and the people who are more shy something to refer to as they are talking. Another practice is to respond to the talkative person who speaks up again by saying, "Let's try to get some other voices in now." Equal participation is hard to achieve, must be explicitly stated as a goal, and requires everyone's cooperation. Moreover, I have found that this is not only something that pounce-free zones require, but also something they facilitate.

I have no illusions that we can transform the public square in its entirety into such a pounce-free zone , but I do think that we can create such spaces on a smaller scale. Within congregations and in collaboration among organizations, we can foster environments where people can wrestle with their different perspectives and with the tensions internal to their own positions.

Conclusion

Admitting that moral ambiguity is a constant companion does not mean that we do nothing about it. This is analogous to Jesus' observation that the poor will always be with us. The implication is that we will always have work to do on their behalf, not that we should do nothing to care for them. Moral ambiguity suggests that our moral reflection must continue, that our positions may need to be revised and always need further development, and that we may have supplementary tasks to undertake alongside the advocacy of our position.

I thoroughly believe that moral ambiguity has moral value. Though it is inconvenient and complicating, moral ambiguity is not a bad thing. Primarily, moral ambiguity sensitizes us to the perspectives of others in a way that inhibits demonizing the individual with whom we disagree. Moreover, attention to the mournful element of even our most certain decision prevents a kind of self-righteous absolutism. When we recognize some truth in the other person's position and renounce our claim to the absolute correctness of our own position, we open up a space for relationship and perhaps reconciliation. If faith enters the public square to buttress absolute positions and reify division, it makes no constructive contribution. But faith can also enter the public square in a different way, with an honest admission of the doubt accompanying decision, with attention to the mournful element of each act, with acknowledgement of the deep humanity of the one who thinks differently, and with an eye on the common good. If we bring faith into the public square in this way, it just might have a transformative effect.

CHAPTER THREE

Theological Humility

A Call for Theological Humility over Dogmatism

Recall that the immediate context for this book is a public square in which people are using religion as they vie for political power. By *public square*, I mean any place where people with different sources of authority meet to discuss issues that affect other people as well. The ultimate move in such a context is to claim divine endorsement for one's political position. This is what the religious right did so effectively in the 1980s and 1990s, and it is what some on the religious left are doing today. In an effort to effect sociopolitical change, we claim divine endorsement for our party, our candidate, or our platform. And even those of us who eschew some partisan theology continue to argue that God does indeed have a political platform and that it, not surprisingly, looks like our own. We may argue that "God is neither a Republican nor a Democrat," but we still claim to know and to advocate "God's politics."[1]

Now, let me be very clear about this contentious point. As I stated in the introduction, the conviction that faith must be socially engaged (and thus not private, individualistic, or otherworldly) is a core commitment of mine. I would not remain a Christian nor would I devote my professional life to teaching Christian ethics if I did not think that bringing this faith tradition to life in the world can make it a more peaceful and just place.

I think that Christians are called to be "disciples of Christ, and not just admirers of Christ," as Bishop Gene Robinson preaches. That is, we must put our faith into action and work to transform the world through bold acts of love and courageous acts for justice. I believe we must advocate for the least advantaged, listen to and stand with the marginalized, and respond to the needs of the most vulnerable members of our population.

I also believe that the Gospel narratives, following the prophetic tradition in the Hebrew Scriptures, provide us with images of the world we are called to realize, a flourishing people and planet. I do not understand this vision to be a distant kingdom, something that arrives at the end of time or in another realm. Rather, I understand this *kin*-dom of God to be an emergent reality, something that is coming to be in every act of kindness, in every moment of reconciliation, in every expression of love. Our job is not, therefore, to wait for divine intervention, nor to compromise these Christian ideals to fit a fixed reality, but rather to work faithfully and diligently to participate in the ongoing transformation of this world into the kin-dom of God.[2]

These faith convictions are deeply meaningful and truly binding for me, but they do not inform my political engagement on their own. In fact, they do not even exist "on their own." There is Scripture to support these claims, and there is a historical trajectory in which to root them. But the movement from text and tradition to this bundle of convictions is by no means a neutral or linear one. We do not craft a faith by simply turning on a tap. Rather, we participate in the construction of our faith in all kinds of ways. Some texts speak to us and to our situation more than others, and we turn to them again and again such that they become a canon within a canon. Changing experiences and circumstances prompt us to interpret the texts differently so that their meaning and import vary. We distinguish (sometimes haphazardly) between contextualized information in biblical narratives and timeless truths that transcend the text. We participate in a community of faith that reinforces some elements of the historical tradition and reconstructs or discards others, affecting the spiritual practices through which we express and attend to our faith.

From this complex and dynamic process, we arrive at a variety of moral positions that we often express with a startling amount of certainty. I observe that the intensity of this rhetoric of certainty is directly proportional to one's sense of threat, the heatedness of the debate, and the size of one's audience. For example, in classroom contexts where students feel safe and are encouraged to wrestle with difficult questions and to deliberate even the hottest topics with supportive dialogue rather than contentious debate, the rhetoric of certitude is minimal. However, in a public square or other kinds of classrooms where one's values, personhood, and loved ones seem under attack, that rhetoric of certitude skyrockets. We express positions rooted in faith as though they are rooted in fact. We reference God's will as though it is only known to us and objectively obtained by us. In this context, where we work so hard to defend values, principles, and people dear to us, our faith morphs into dogma and apologetics.

The purpose of this chapter is to argue for theological humility even in—indeed especially in—the public square. I use the phrase *theological humility* to denote a posture that (1) admits limitations of knowledge and partiality of perspective, (2) explicitly and deliberately practices hermeneutics, and (3) remains transparent about faith commitments and accountable to other sources of knowledge. What does this posture look and sound like? First of all, admitting the limitations of our knowledge and the partiality of our perspective means that we no longer equate our interpretation of God's will with God's will. We make no claims to objective knowledge of God's will, but take responsibility for the subjective role in discernment. "God wants" becomes "I believe that the fullest expression of God's love is. . . ;" "God says" becomes "I think that Jesus' mandate to care for the poor means we must . . ." This does not mean that we become thoroughly agnostic or that we stop articulating and acting upon our discernment of God's will. But it does mean that we know that there is a difference between God's will and our discernment of it, and that we act and speak accordingly.

The statement, "This is my interpretation of God's will," is always the *starting point* for critical reflection and for conversation. We err when we use such statements to rest on our laurels or to foreclose dialogue. Admitting the role of subjectivity in discernment—admitting that we do not access God's will in the same way that we look up a telephone number—means that we also have a greater responsibility to interpret *well*. Fortunately, contemporary Christian theology has devoted considerable attention to the study of interpretation, or hermeneutics. Hermeneutics draws our attention to the lenses through which we see the world. My theology teacher, Sallie McFague, explained the process to her students this way: I am admiring a landscape when I realize that I am looking through a window; so, I begin to examine the window and the ways in which it shapes my view of the landscape. Hermeneutical practices focus our attention on the process of our interpretation, making this process more deliberate and self-critical.

The second feature of our theological humility—practicing hermeneutics—sounds like a series of questions. Why do you select this passage as authoritative over another? Why do you interpret that passage as you do? What are the commitments that you bring to the text? How do your understanding of God and your experience in this changing world inform one another? And, turning these questions back on ourselves makes this a mutual inquiry rather than an inquisition. Hermeneutics, as a practice of theological humility, sounds like an honest exchange between people who support each other's efforts to live faithfully. This posture also looks like hard work, which it is. It takes constant effort in the form of study, conversation, and critical reflection to ensure that one's interpretation of God's will is not haphazard or self-serving.

Third, theological humility refuses to use faith as a trump card in matters of public policy. In this posture, I am transparent about the many commitments that inform me, including those rooted in a particular religious tradition. But I am also clear about the extensions that I must craft between these faith commitments (which come in the form of general mandates or in the particular expression of a distant culture and time) and the particular policies that I debate. Let me offer an analogy to explain this point.

I live in a canyon neighborhood where several houses protrude from the sides of the mountain, supported by massive stilts and beams. Walking beneath one such house on a path like we frequently do, I am consistently impressed by the construction. You can see the portion of the foundation that is built directly onto the mountain, but the flooring then extends at least forty feet beyond the earth, with the stilts extending down another thirty feet to touch the earth again. Clearly, all parts of the house meet the mountain at some point, but the house itself is not supported only by the earth. Bracketing the ecological questions around such construction, it is clear that the stilts and beams are essential to the house. Although the earth provides the ultimate foundation, no one could honestly say that the whole house is supported only by the mountain. We see the stilts. We also see the point where the floor leaves the earth and extends out supported by the stilts and beams. The stilts and beams are necessary to connect the earth to the floor. Indeed, the earth cannot provide support to the house without the stilts and beams.

Theological humility means that we see our faith-informed politics as analogous to this house. Theology and sacred text certainly inform and support the house, but we cannot honestly say that the whole house is supported by faith alone. We can say that our politics, like every aspect of our life, is rooted ultimately in God. But we must also acknowledge the stilts and beams that we utilize to connect a theological conviction to a political position. The stilts and beams may come in the form of another source of information discussed in chapter 2, such as scientific data, political philosophy, economic theory, personal experience, or historical analogy. So, building on the previous two features of theological humility, we must admit the contingencies of our theological convictions and also debate the merits of social and political policies that we believe give those convictions their fullest expression.

Like moral ambiguity, theological humility complicates Christians' political activism, a concern I will address later in this chapter. But first, I must say that such complication is worthwhile and important because of the specter of religious authoritarianism. Like other forms of authoritarianism, this one demands unquestioned obedience, dismisses all other sources of knowledge, and denies legitimacy to all other positions. Religious authoritarianism is antithetical to democratic discourse, enslaves individual conscience, and facilitates violence against people who hold contrary religious and philosophical positions. We pave the way for religious authoritarianism whenever we insist that we alone know the will of God, that our knowledge of God's will is beyond the reach of critical inquiry, and that divine endorsement for a particular policy trumps any other considerations about it.

Christians who want to express faith in the public square must find ways to do so without importing an "external authority" to which all other persons and views must be subject. But more than that, Christians must bring faith into public spaces as one voice among many, one participant in the discussion. When entering the public square, faith must take a seat at the table and relinquish its claim to a podium.

One characteristic of public spaces must be underscored, namely the presence of different sources of authority. It is not only that diverse people with different positions interact here, but also that these people are informed by and committed to different authoritative sources. I cannot expect others to accept my faith commitments as authoritative, no matter how deeply I hold them. In this heterogeneous public space, statements of faith constitute the beginning of a conversation, never the final word. Having faith take a seat at the table means that we decide to engage the substance of each position rather than offering its source of authority as the justification for it.

This does not, however, require us to leave faith out of the conversation. In truth, mine is the opposite position. We should not only bring faith in, but also articulate it fully and with as much transparency as possible. This is really a simple point: if we are going to bring faith into heterogeneous, public spaces, then we must be willing to subject faith to the processes of open dialogue. We must be prepared to explain how we arrive at a certain faith stance and how that stance supports a particular position. Such practices are made even more crucial by the fact that faith is not only a source of authority, but also part of our reasoning about the substance of contentious issues. We must think clearly about the role faith plays, and we must be willing to discuss our discernment in the course of open dialogue and critical inquiry. Theological humility is the disposition that makes such engagement possible.

Admit Limitations of Knowledge and Partiality of Perspective

Theological humility begins with the statement that all knowledge is conditioned by the standpoint of the knower. What we see, even through the eyes of faith, is shaped by where we sit. We do not have objective knowledge of God or objective access to God's will. What we know is mediated through text, tradition, communities of faith, and personal experience. Clearly this position raises questions about the meaning of revelation and the authority of Scripture. I will address the question about revelation at this point and turn to the question of Scripture in the following, related discussion of hermeneutics.

Like every aspect of this book, the matter of revelation alone warrants volumes. So, let me refine the concern as much as possible before proceeding. Part of the rationale for theological humility is the specter of religious authoritarianism and the insistence that no single authority should trump other sources of knowledge or enslave the individual conscience. This concern was forcefully articulated by German Protestant male theologians working in the wake of the Enlightenment, which celebrated human capacities for reason and freedom of conscience. Their proposal included subjecting all authoritative sources (including Scripture, revelation, and tradition) to critical inquiry to see which claims could withstand the test of reason. Theologian George Stroup succinctly captures the implication of this turn to reason: "No longer were revealed truths the final arbiter; now human reason became the final court of appeal for the interpretation of reality."[3]

It is true that establishing reason as the "final court of appeal" enables it to function in an authoritarian manner. This is particularly problematic when reason is narrowly construed as a rational human faculty that enables us to deliberate a question without recourse to personal viewpoint or subjective inclination. The starting point for theological humility—that all knowledge is conditioned by the standpoint of the knower—applies to reason as well. Thus I do not intend to subjugate faith to a "rational authoritarianism," but rather to encourage humility in all of our assertions of truth, regardless of the sources that inform them. All knowledge is partial; all perspectives are limited.

To return to the question, then, what role does revelation play? Or, more exactly, how can we understand, speak of, and reference revelation with humility? As Stroup writes, "Revelation means an unveiling or, to use a more contemporary idiom, a 'disclosure.' When revelation takes place a veil is dropped, and that which had been masked or hidden from view is disclosed."[4] By definition, it is an insight gained in a rather mysterious way; that is, we do not tend to think of revelation as something that we reason ourselves toward. It is, rather, something that comes to us. And it is, truthfully, the most modest of suggestions to say that we must begin by acknowledging that *all* is not revealed to us and that which *is* revealed is partial and incomplete. In a very real sense, my call for theological humility is not an attack on the meaning of revelation, but a return to it.

In order for us to bring revelation into the public square, we must accompany it with reason, and we must understand reason to be much broader than the rational faculty mentioned above. One assumption about reason that succeeding generations have appropriately disputed is its claim to objective or somehow "pure" knowledge. This assumption is faulty in at least two ways. First, it assumes that we can reason apart from our experience, that we can think about the world without considering our location in it. Second, it discounts all other sources of knowledge, such as experience, emotion, and imagination. What we need is a broader concept of reason, one that includes these other sources of knowledge rather than discounting them. The shift here is parallel to that which I recommended in the previous chapter, from deliberation to discernment. I advocate this shift by standing on the shoulders of a generation of feminists who have effectively criticized the feasibility and the desirability of this "disembodied" thinker and employed for a more inclusive epistemology. However, feminists have not been alone in asserting this kind of change. Consider, for example, this profoundly beautiful passage from H. Richard Niebuhr's, *Meaning of Revelation*, published in 1941.

> A strange blindness often afflicts those who believe that they employ the strictly impersonal and descriptive method in all affairs of life; they do not see how they abandon this method themselves in every decision to publish their ideas and in all their identifications of themselves with their thoughts. The participant in life simply cannot escape thinking in terms of persons and of values. It would be possible to do so only if he could depersonalize the self, become a body without an inner life, without joys and sorrows, loves and hates, without neighbors, without hope or fear—a thing in a world of things.[5]

To increase the cooperation between reason and revelation, Niebuhr utilized the concept of "practical reason," by which he meant "the reason of a self rather than of impersonal mind."[6] Such reason does not discount revelation, but is truly a help to it because it interprets an "otherwise inscrutable sensation."[7] This point about interpretation relates more broadly to H. Richard Niebuhr's epistemology, which insists that we interpret every piece of data we receive, no matter where it comes from. That process of interpretation helps us to make meaning of experiences, information, and sensations. We simply cannot make sense of our world without interpretation, which means that revelation needs reason. In Niebuhr's words, "The heart must reason; the participating self cannot escape the necessity of looking for pattern and meaning in its life and relations."[8]

Niebuhr understood the relationship between reason and revelation to be mutually beneficial. Reason helps us to interpret revelation, and revelation provides understanding. When we speak of revelation, he wrote, "we point to that occasion in our history which enables us to understand."[9] "By revelation in our history, then, we mean that special occasion which provides us with an image by means of which all the occasions of personal and common life become intelligible."[10] In making this point, Niebuhr describes revelation itself as rational, "because it makes the understanding of order and meaning in personal history possible."[11] Niebuhr did not view revelation as a supernatural set of timeless truths imparted periodically to human beings, but rather as "simply historic faith."[12] Revelation, for Niebuhr, is a faith community's interpretation of its experience unfolding in history, an interpretation rendered intelligible by the narrative of that particular faith community. For Christians, revelation is the stories gathered in Scripture and elsewhere that help us to understand who we are as participants in this historic community. Revelation "makes our past intelligible," helps the heart to "remember what it had forgotten" and to understand it, and provides a common history for a disparate community.[13] Revelation is therefore not only a source of historical understanding, but also a requisite for self-knowledge.

This emphasis on the community of meaning relates to Niebuhr's observation that "all knowledge is conditioned by the standpoint of the knower."[14] He then clarifies that this standpoint is informed by history and by culture. We are "social human beings whose reason is . . . qualified by inheritance from a particular society," and we are "historical selves whose [knowledge and ways of knowing] . . . are limited, moving and changing in time." Niebuhr continues,

> This self-knowledge has not come easily to us; we have resisted it and continue to avoid it when we can, but the cumulative evidence of history and sociology continue to impress upon us, against our desire, the conviction that our reason is not only in space-time but that time-space is in our reason. The patterns and models we employ to understand the historical world may have had a heavenly origin, but as we know and use them they are, like ourselves, creatures of history and time; though we direct our thought to eternal and transcendent beings, it is not eternal transcendent; though we regard the universal, the image of the universal in our mind is not a universal image.[15]

These comments reinforce the critique of objective or pure reason mentioned earlier. They also map crucial middle ground between the false dichotomy of objective knowledge and sheer relativism. In his mediating style (that I so appreciate and that drives many of my students crazy), Niebuhr argues that acknowledging our standpoint does not negate the knowledge we have from it. "It is not evident that the man who is forced to confess that his view of things is conditioned by the standpoint he occupies must doubt the reality of what he sees. It is not apparent that one who knows that his concepts are not universal must also doubt that they are concepts of the universal."[16]

To say that all knowledge is conditioned, limited, and partial is not to say we have no knowledge. But it is to say that our knowledge of something is not equivalent to that something. I cannot equate my partial knowledge of the universe to the universe itself. I know/see a piece of it, but not the whole thing. And, more to the point of this book, my knowledge of God's will is not the same thing as God's will. This argument is foundational to theological humility. What I believe, what I discern, what I know about the will of God is not the same thing as the will of God. And as H. Richard Niebuhr so forcefully and consistently argued, to claim otherwise—to reduce God's will to my limited discernment of it— is idolatry. Theological humility, beginning with acknowledgement of standpoint, is an essential practice of faith itself.

Thus far, I have described this first feature of theological humility in negative terms, as the admission of limited knowledge. However, there is a constructive practice that corresponds to this admission as well, namely the necessity of dialogue. In H. Richard Niebuhr's work, one finds frequent reference to the importance of "companion knowers," historical figures or contemporary persons against whom we examine our interpretations and verify our experience.[17] Acknowledging our standpoint propels us into conversation with others if we are to gain a more complete perspective. With theological humility, we enter into this conversation not with a dogmatic grasp of truth, but open to (and in need of) the insights of others.

Explicitly and Deliberately Practice Hermeneutics

The larger question of revelation provides helpful background to the related question of the meaning and authority of Scripture. Not only is Scripture considered a source of revelation, but also the authority of Scripture was similarly challenged by post Enlightenment thinkers. Gary Dorrien, author of *The Making of American Liberal Theology*, describes their challenge this way:

The essential idea of liberal theology is that all claims to truth, in theology as in other disciplines, must be made on the basis of reason and experience, not by appeal to external authority. Christian scripture may be recognized as spiritually authoritative within Christian experience, but its word does not settle or establish truth claims about matters of fact.[18]

How then do we think about Scripture, if not as external authority that transcends critical inquiry and trumps other sources of knowledge? We understand and approach Scripture as historical documents that reflect a particular context and bear the marks of generations of interpretation, translation, and canonization. We approach the Bible, then, as we do other ancient manuscripts, attentive to the culture in which the stories were recorded and aware of the complex process of development from papyri to canon.

This historical-critical method of biblical study is related to the history of religions approach, which nineteenth century liberal theologians applied to Christianity and all religions. In the words of theologian Dorothee Soelle, the history of religions approach "means that all writings, all confessions of faith, dogmas, all church constitutions, expressions of piety, Christian customs, prayers, came into being in history."[19] Theologians engaging this historical method understood themselves as involved in a type of revolution, primarily against the dogmatic method, which had effectively kept human reason subservient. Nineteenth century theologian Ernst Troeltsch described the revolution this way:

Everywhere the older absolutistic or dogmatic approach, which regarded particular conditions and ideas as simply "given" and therefore absolutized them into unchangeable norms, is being supplanted by the historical approach, which regards even those matters that are alleged to be most obviously "given" and those powers that control the largest number of people as having been produced by the flow of history.[20]

Contemporaries of Troeltsch and subsequent generations have argued that through the historical method, "Scriptures and their Jesus seemed to lose their claim to absoluteness and even any claim to special force of obligation."[21] Among progressive Christians, we find those who appreciate and practice the historical method and value its leveling effect on Christianity and its facilitation of religious tolerance. We also find those who believe that the lineage of historicism has weakened the prophetic power of the Christian faith, and that those who remain under the power of historicism fail to "take the Bible seriously."[22]

Revisiting the debate between Troeltsch and Adolf von Harnack may clarify our present situation a bit. Harnack and Troeltsch were students of Albrecht Ritschl, the founder of the history of religions school of thought.[23] For many of us in the field of Christian ethics, Ritschl is the taproot of liberal theological ethics because he not only advanced the history of religions approach, but also focused intently on the ethical implications of the faith. Indeed, he persistently argued that Christianity is an ethical religion, meaning that it is not primarily a doctrine, but rather "a way of living, a style of life expressed in ethical vocation."[24]

Ritschl's two students, Harnack and Troeltsch (who were later colleagues as well), reflected on the ethical teaching within the faith tradition and the reality of its historical development, and they debated whether one could identify teachings that transcend their context and thus constitute the "essence of the faith." Harnack answered affirmatively and worked to trace a "red thread"[25] running through the history of the Christian religion. He undertook this investigation and advanced his own affirmative response in *What Is Christianity?* Recognizing the historicity of the text, Harnack describes two possible responses and makes clear his preference: "Either the Gospel is in all respects identical with its earliest form, in which case it came with its time and has departed with it; or else it contains something which, under differing historical forms, is of permanent validity. The latter is the true view."[26] So, Harnack set about "distinguishing what is permanent from what is fleeting, what is rudimentary from what is merely historical."[27] He concludes that the essential feature of Christianity is the love commandment and the corresponding call to union, solidarity, and charity. In his own words,

> You observe how Jesus felt the material wants of the poor, and how he deduced a remedy for such distress from the commandment: "Love thy neighbor as thyself." . . . It is not only that the Gospel preaches solidarity and the helping of others; it is in this message that its real import consists. . . . Its tendency to union and brotherliness is not so much an accidental phenomenon in its history as the essential feature of its character. . . . The Gospel is a social message, solemn and over-powering in its force; it is the proclamation of solidarity and brotherliness, in favour of the poor.[28]

Troeltsch disagreed with Harnack in a few different ways, although he shared Harnack's historical approach to the Bible, which turns not to dogma and church institution, but to Jesus' actual life and teachings, as recorded by his followers.[29] However, he expressed concern with the ethical implications of naming such an essence. Troeltsch's concerns are, to my mind, precursors to liberationist hermeneutics of suspicion. Who identifies the essence? What is excluded? On what grounds? His point was that identifying an essence is not a neutral activity; it is laden with the presuppositions of the person making the claim.[30] Rather than stripping Christianity down to its essence, Troeltsch argued that we should consider it in its entirety. Christianity is not a skeleton, but a living and fluctuating organism, and we must work to understand it in all of its variety. In his words, "The essence of Christianity can only be arrived at in so far as Christianity is thought of as a part of an overall religious and cultural development."[31]

Troeltsch engaged in this study with his two-volume work, *Social Teaching of the Christian Churches*, an examination of the ways in which Christian communities, from the early church through the eighteenth century, understood and applied the ethical teachings conveyed in the Gospels. From this study, he advanced a particular understanding of Christian ethics as ongoing negotiation between the ideals of the faith and the changing socio-historical circumstances. He did not envision a neat or straightforward application from faith to situation, but a process involving dynamic and mutually influential interplay between faith and history. Not only does faith inform my interpretation of history, but I also understand faith differently in light of historical experiences. Consequently, the ideal of faith is not "picked up each time" and applied in a neutral way, but rather "every time it is newly created."[32]

The debate between Harnack and Troeltsch sheds light on one aspect of "the divided mind of the religious left."[33] Some of us keep an eye on the red thread of love, solidarity, and charity (to maintain Harnack's language), arguing that these essential Christian commitments persist and must be embodied in every time and place. Yes, say others, like me, who lean more closely toward Troeltsch, but the exact expression of these enduring commitments varies according to context. The commandment to neighbor-love does not lead all of us to the same actions or positions, which means that referencing the commandment is not a sufficient explanation for my position. (Nor is it a sufficient criticism of a different position.) The movement from an enduring value of the faith to its expression in concrete terms of behavior, position, and policy is a complex one, and there are variables that we must account for.

This does not mean that Christianity—even understood as a historical development—has no enduring values, but it does suggest that incarnating the value in a particular place and time and with reference to particular people and policies gives it a highly contextualized expression. We can certainly make the case that the contextualized expression (in the form of a public policy, for example) is the best approximation of solidarity with the poor. But we cannot argue that a particular piece of legislation is *the* Christian position. To say that faith informs a position does not make the position the only expression of the faith.

An analogy may be helpful: My daughter and I each have a glass of water. I put an instant tea mix in mine, and she puts lemonade mix in hers. I say, "Look, your water is not water anymore!" And she says, "Neither is yours!" We practice theological humility by acknowledging the difference between water and tea and lemonade, and by clarifying (for ourselves and others) the methods by which we move from water to tea or lemonade, from enduring value to contextualized expression. That is, theological humility requires deliberate and explicit hermeneutical practices. The following pages offer examples of hermeneutical practices used by some contemporary Christian ethicists. I am not recommending one of these practices over others; but I am commending this kind of hermeneutical self-awareness. We need to do more than insist that the tea is of water, and the lemonade is not. We need to pay attention to the way we make tea, and we need to be prepared to explain that process to others and to ask them to do the same.

Recall the image of the window referenced earlier, for this is one starting point for hermeneutical practice, namely attention to the window through which we observe the world, the experiences with which we interpret a text. We cannot approach a text without our own experience anymore than we can live in the world without our bodies. Although this argument continues to find resistance in a variety of places, it is well established by now. Twenty years ago, Rosemary Radford Ruether argued that

> human experience is both the starting point and the ending point of the circle of interpretation. Codified tradition both reaches back to its roots in experience and is constantly renewed through the test of experience. Experience includes experience of the divine and experience of oneself, in relationship to society and the world, in an interacting dialectic.[34]

We practice theological humility by articulating our experience and owning its effect on our interpretations of Scripture and the circumstances to which we apply it. This hermeneutical practice is not an option, in my view. The following four are, however, offered as examples, not mandates.

Sometimes, we approach Scripture thematically. We believe that a given theme is true to the nature of God, core to Jesus' teaching, or otherwise essential to the Christian faith. And we use that theme as a filtering mechanism against particular passages or other interpretations. The theme not only helps us to interpret passages, but also becomes a criterion according to which we measure the truthfulness of a given text and determine the extent to which it has authority over us. Now, clearly this is not a fundamentalist approach: it does not assume that the Bible in its entirety is the Word of God and completely binding. Rather, it assumes that the Bible represents a collection of material recorded by human beings, and that this material includes some timeless truths that are binding and some historical mandates that are not. And, we determine which is which with reference to these themes or "prominent lines."[35]

Suppose, for example, I interpret Scripture according to the theme of freedom. God is a God of freedom, and the red thread running through the texts is that of liberation. Thus, the truthful and binding passages are those that liberate humankind rather than subjugate and oppress. Similar themes could include love and hope; dissimilar themes that nonetheless function similarly include judgment and election. Interpretation along the lines of love recognizes the presence of violent imagery in Scripture, and questions the truthfulness of such passages because they are inconsistent with a loving God. Interpretation along the lines of judgment makes use of such passages to caution those who seek salvation. Even those who reject the idea of distinguishing between those passages that are truthful and binding and those that are not most likely have themes that they use to interpret Scripture and to privilege some passages over others. Acknowledging the themes or prominent lines that shape our interpretation of Scripture is a practice in theological humility.

Margaret Farley, the Roman Catholic feminist I quoted earlier, describes a similar practice that clarifies the role of core commitments in our selection and interpretation of Scripture, commitments that also challenge claims to scriptural authority. We approach Scripture with deeply held commitments, "convictions so basic that to contradict them would be to experience violence done to the integrity of the self."[36] It is crucial to hear Farley's point that these are not casual commitments. She is speaking of "the kind of conviction so basic to a person's understanding that a contradictory witness cannot be believed without doing violence to one's self."[37] Her examples include a belief in fundamental human equality or the belief "that women are fully human and are to be valued as such."[38] These convictions serve a selective and interpretive purpose for Scripture and for all other sources we might bring into ethical deliberation. That is, we utilize material that is consonant with these deeply held convictions and we challenge the truthfulness of that which is not. Clarifying our deeply held commitments and rejecting that which transgresses them and does violence to us is a liberating practice. And, articulating these commitments and their influence on our interpretation is a practice of theological humility. It is also crucial to note that this is a practice that those seeking liberation from oppressive forms of religion and socialization have undertaken, while those in dominant positions claim to take all of the Bible as it is.

The last two examples come from recent publications in Christian ethics, *Disruptive Christian Ethics* by Traci West and *Kingdom Ethics* by Glen Stassen and David Gushee. Both of these texts offer examples of a hermeneutical approach to the particular content of Scripture. Indeed, West purposefully presents her approach as an alternative to the thematic method mentioned earlier. She writes,

> When scripture's moral meaning is sought, its universality is most highly valued because it does not seem to be contingent upon the details of the present circumstances or bound to the particular ancient cultural context in which the scripture was written. But the cultural particularities that inform the scripture passages make a difference in the theological and ethical meaning of the text.[39]

She then explores the particularities of the Magnificat as recorded in the Gospel of Luke.

> Mary's insistent words in the Magnificat carry a message about God's concern for the particular lives and needs of the lowly and poor. . . . Furthermore, in the canticle, salvation of this particular group, the lowly and the poor, is linked with the salvation of the broader faith community of Israel.[40]

West goes on to explore the ways in which this close reading of the Magnificat might inform one's response to single black mothers receiving public assistance and to the ways in which these women have been abused by the rhetoric of public policy.[41] West makes us cognizant of the differences that a close reading can make. She also raises the importance of careful biblical exegesis. If we are going to utilize Scripture in our moral deliberation, we must make sure that we understand the text on its own terms and in its own context. The difference between the contexts of the text and our own place and time must not be an excuse for overlooking details. Nor should it require a more universal approach, through which we only work at the level of themes, general values, and more universal-sounding mandates. As West notes, "In this search for the universal ethical point that must be separated from scriptural particularities, many possibilities for intellectual stimulation, spiritual nurture, and social change can be lost."[42] Studying and wrestling with the socio-historical particularities of the text is also a practice of theological humility.

Stassen and Gushee illustrate a Christ-centered hermeneutic. After reviewing a number of approaches to Scripture, they look to the historical Jesus to see how he utilized his own religious tradition. They note, for example, that he approached the teachings of the Hebrew Bible as covenant, not law, and in a prophetic rather than a legalistic way.[43] But, more fundamentally, they argue that he began with Scripture, though he did not discount tradition. Jesus "clearly cherished the Jewish religious tradition and participated in it in a wide variety of ways. But he insisted on subjecting that tradition to Scripture and to God's creative and redemptive intentions, sifting out what did not survive such a test."[44] Stassen and Gushee take Jesus' own ethical method as instructive and argue for the "supremacy of Scripture as the central authoritative source for Christian ethics."[45]

> We say yes to *sola scriptura* if that means that Scripture is the only authoritative and fully trustworthy source of authority for

Christian ethics. The insights gained from all other sources must be sifted and interpreted by Scripture and must be rejected if they conflict with Scripture. The Bible is the "sun" around which all other sources of authority are brought into orbit.[46]

From the argument for the primacy of Scripture and with their Christ-centered hermeneutic, Stassen and Gushee describe a three-step process for interpretation specifically and moral deliberation more broadly.

Look first to Jesus—examining his incarnation/death/resurrection and his life/ministry/teachings.

Read all other Scriptures through the prophetic interpretive grid that Jesus employed and in light of all that we know of Jesus' witness on this issue.

Then look to other sources of authority for help on the basis of the same interpretive grid, remembering that Jesus is alive and continues to instruct his church through the witness of the Holy Spirit (Jn 15).[47]

Here, we have a process of hermeneutics that utilizes a series of concentric circles. We begin in the center circle focused on the life and teachings of Jesus. We then utilize that material to interpret the surrounding material in the prophetic tradition. And then we look to other sources of knowledge, interpreted through the prophetic grid, with the belief that these other sources can also be revelatory in some sense. It seems important to note that the inner circles shape the interpretation of the outer ones so that we are clear about the direction of influence here. It is purposefully and in many senses Christo-centric, and it relies on very careful study of Jesus' life and the meaning of his teachings in the context of his own culture. The following section contrasts with Stassen and Gushee's emphasis on the primacy of Scripture, which I do not share. However, I do see their explicit and deliberate hermeneutical method as a practice of theological humility.

Transparency about Faith and Accountability to Other Sources of Knowledge

As we move into the public square, we must be transparent about the faith commitments we bring with us *and* about the processes through which we come to them. The third aspect of theological humility, however, argues that *sola fides*—by faith alone—is not an acceptable argument in the public square. We must also understand the issues on their own terms and be able to justify our positions in the language of other relevant sources of knowledge. Moreover, in order for our religious and political selves to remain integrated, we need to strive for consonance between the conclusions of faith and those reached via these other sources of knowledge. When dissonance persists, we need to re-evaluate our positions and the sources that inform them, including faith. My position is that faith must never be the only reason to advocate for a position; nor should it trump other sources of knowledge.

This position stands in the tradition of liberal theology, which has historically called for "reasonableness in religion." Although I do not use that language, I do believe that claims of faith must be accountable to other sources of knowledge. Particularly as faith enters into the public square, it must give up privilege. In this space, faith is one source of knowledge among many, which means that it is also subject to re-evaluation in light of other positions. The liberal theology that informs my position has been frequently criticized by some progressive Christians, and I will address some of the relevant concerns as I proceed.

My proposal for transparency and accountability owes much to Franklin Gamwell's 2004 text, *Politics as a Christian Vocation*.[48] Gamwell locates himself firmly in the liberal tradition, advocates reason as a test for validity of all claims, and argues that reason must be the arbiter in pluralistic societies if they are to remain democratic. Democracy requires "full and free political discussion and debate [which is to say] politics by the way of reason; only those political claims that can be validated in reasoned discourse should direct the decisions or activities of the state."[49] Gamwell argues that democratic political participation is part of the Christian vocation; and yet participation in such debate requires that Christians submit "their own belief about ultimate worth, like any other, to validation or invalidation by argument."[50]

Gamwell recognizes that submitting such beliefs to the test of reason is a departure from the "majority voice" in the Christian tradition, one that argues "that true belief about God and human salvation cannot be fully validated independently of God's self-disclosure through Jesus Christ and the scriptural witness to it."[51] However, for Gamwell, this limitation to reason also precludes a Christian's participation in political debate. "Making a political claim, including one that contests another claim, is a communicative act in which one pledges to any recipient that one's claim can be validated or redeemed by argument and, therefore, also concedes that one's claim may be invalidated in the same way."[52] I cannot fully participate in such discourse if I declare my deepest commitments to be out of bounds for debate or otherwise immune to criticism. Thus, for Gamwell, the only way for Christians to participate in politics—and thus fulfill this vocation—is to be willing to subject all claims to this communicative process.

I appreciate Gamwell's description of democracy as a communicative process that requires participants' willingness to subject their views to debate. This description crystallizes the connection between theological humility and democracy, because participation in this communicative process of critical inquiry is a practice of theological humility. Thus, Gamwell helps me to argue that democracy requires theological humility (giving us a political argument to accompany the theological one advanced through the discussion of revelation earlier in this chapter). Indeed, bringing faith into politics without submitting it to open, critical discourse is a form of authoritarianism.

My position does differ from Gamwell's in one significant way, however. Gamwell believes that faith can be validated by reason, and I expect there to be unresolved tensions between the two. I reserve space in the life of faith for convictions that reason cannot validate. However, if/when we bring one of those convictions to bear on a public matter, then we must hold it accountable to other sources of knowledge. This means that my faith needs to answer to the scientific view, the political stance, the historical development, or the personal experience that calls it into question. Gamwell's description of a communicative process holds here as well. But the nature of the process I envision (and experience) is less like rational discourse and more like heart-felt dialogue. Moreover, I understand this process to be ongoing, just like the processes of moral discernment described in the previous chapter. Theological humility requires that faith participate in this process, relinquishing claims to special authority.

We find another model for public faith in a 2004 text by Christian ethicist Thomas Ogletree, titled *The World Calling*. He describes a process of multiple layers of translation from the context of the Bible to our own context, and from the language of the Christian tradition into the language of a broader public. Thus he argues:

> When Christians attempt to reconstruct their traditions in their bearing on the resolution of difficult social problems in a secular,

religiously plural society, they have to recast insights derived from their traditions in forms appropriate to the society's public life. . . . To speak to contemporary public issues, the churches must learn to articulate the salient features of their own distinctive witness in relation to values broadly shared within the body politic.[53]

Ogletree and I are saying slightly different things, though their actual effect is similar. Ogletree encourages Christians to be multilingual so that we can translate our convictions into the language of the broader society. I think it is important to articulate our faith commitments in their own language and to explain the processes of faith by which we reach them. This is what I mean by being transparent about our faith. However, because I do not think we should stop there, my position becomes more similar to Ogletree's. I believe that we must also seek consonance between the content of faith commitments and that derived from other sources of knowledge.

Seeking consonance and performing translation are similar, it seems to me. The difference is that my model keeps the language of faith in the open as we strive to find and articulate consonance. In translation, the language of faith is replaced with secular discourse. A second difference is that *striving* for consonance assumes the possibility that dissonance will persist. When this happens, we may reevaluate the faith commitment and continue striving, or we may struggle with moral ambiguity caused by our sense of an incompatibility between, for example, the requirements of faith and the realities of history. However, theological humility does not allow us to use faith as a trump card in these moments.

There are some concerns about liberal theology generally that apply to this third feature of theological humility and thus warrant attention. First, many argue that the test of reason (or accountability to other sources of knowledge) so limits the sphere of authority for Christian sources that it privatizes the faith altogether. If

Christian sources—Scripture, tradition, revelation—have no authority outside of Christian experience, then the Christian faith has no role to play in public spaces. Restricting the authority of faith effectively "locates religion within the private sphere of civil society."[54] I am not convinced that the choices implied by this criticism are the only ones we have: either faith is authoritative over all other sources of knowledge or it is banished to the private realm. Rather, I think that faith can be a responsible participant in public discourse; that it can join in the conversation without taking it over. Indeed, I think the future of democracy in religiously pluralistic places depends on it.

A second criticism applies to Ogletree's translation and to my consonance-seeking, namely that we are both capitulating to culture. As Delwin Brown argues, liberals who recast their tradition fail "to keep the distinctive resources of the Christian inheritance at the center of their reflection."[55] Liberal theology, he continues,

> went wrong, from a progressive perspective, when reasoning based on (supposedly) common human experience became for them more than valued *tools and tests* to be utilized in shaping the inherited Christian materials; gradually it became also the *source* of liberal theology. As that happened, the historic stories, symbols, ideas, analyses and imperatives of historic Christian faith moved to the dim—and largely optional—margins of liberal Christian reflection. Liberal theology became something more akin to philosophy.[56]

This assessment—that reason becomes the source of liberal theology—gives rise to another way in which this tradition seems to capitulate to culture. It is not only that faith eventually gives way to philosophy, but that reason itself is so closely related to culture that liberal theologians become the "custodians of culture"[57] as well as the defenders of reason.

Critics argue that liberals are so concerned about the reasonableness of our faith and accountability to other sources of information, that our theology loses a counter-cultural edge. Historically, liberal theologians have not only valued reason, but also placed great faith in the "products of reason," meaning advancements in culture, science, industry, and technology that promise to better the human condition. Indeed, as H. Richard Niebuhr explained, reason and culture were intertwined at the root of liberal theology with Kant's assumption that reason "means the particular exercise of man's analytical and synthetic intellectual power characteristic of the best culture of the time."[58] There is a sense here that human reason finds its expression in culture. Liberal theology has, therefore, had a "positive relationship to the cutting edge of the culture," which becomes problematic when much of culture "now seems to cut in the wrong direction," as John Cobb argues.[59]

I share this concern, but I also see the situation differently. I think that this criticism assumes that there is no counter-cultural edge provided through other sources of knowledge with which Christianity might cooperate. And I disagree with this assumption. I believe that "counter-cultural" Christians can find partners in secular movements opposing economic globalization, environmental destruction, and United States imperialism, for example. Arguing that faith should seek consonance in other sources of knowledge does not *necessarily* mean that it capitulates to culture or becomes a defender of the status quo. Again, this concern assumes that Christianity has a monopoly on dissent, which is obviously not the case.

In sum, bringing faith into the public square in a transparent way that also remains accountable to other sources of knowledge means this: We must speak clearly and honestly about the ways in which our faith informs the positions we advocate. We must be able to describe the process by which we reach the positions we do, and this assumes that the process itself is deliberate and careful. We must bring faith into the public square as a participant in the conversation, meaning that it does not enter with special privilege or special force of obligation for others. In my view, we cannot advocate a position in the public square by faith alone. Rather, I believe that theological humility and democratic participation require that we deliberate issues on their own terms and identify other sources of support for the positions we advocate. If we cannot identify any other reason beyond faith to support a position, I think we do need to re-evaluate our faith. I do not agree that this practice of accountability forfeits the prophetic power of the Christian faith, but it does require us to seek out similarly prophetic voices informed by other sources of knowledge, of which there are many.

Conclusion

Theological humility requires that we be transparent about the faith that informs us and clear about the processes through which we determine the social and political implications of our faith. We must also be honest about the limitations of knowledge and partiality of perspective, and open to the ways in which other sources of knowledge can both contribute to our understanding and challenge its truth. More so than in the other chapters, the material on theological humility is deeply informed by the liberal tradition. However, I have not intended a wholesale apology for liberal theology because there are elements of the tradition that I too find problematic. However, the central commitments to critical inquiry of faith, to freedom from all forms of religious authoritarianism, and to a historical understanding of religion warrant vigorous defense. It is a mistake, in my view, for progressive Christians to write off this theological tradition because of its problematic features. After all, progressive Christianity is a part of liberal theology, broadly construed,[60] and there are individuals under the progressive Christian umbrella who identify more closely with liberal theology than with progressive evangelicalism. Moreover, the liberal tradition offers mechanisms for religious participation in democratic discourse and thus constitutes a valuable resource for those of us committed to making faith a participant in heterogeneous public spaces.

I want to conclude by responding to one additional concern about liberal theology, namely that it is "overly intellectual." It is important for me to name this criticism and address it here because this book is filled with calls for careful thinking, study, and critical inquiry. These intellectual invitations reflect more than my own practices and profession; they also reflect the historical relationship between liberal theology in the United States and shifts in theological education that Gary Dorrien describes. "In the early nineteenth century the center of American theological education had passed from the denominational college to the graduate seminary; at the end of the century it began to pass to divinity schools allied with research-oriented universities."[61] This, obviously, does not mean that denominational colleges and free-standing seminaries passed away, but it does mean that theological education also took up residence in a context where liberal theology could flourish, namely the university-related divinity school. Thus, as Dorrien aptly illustrates, liberal theology became a "decidedly academic enterprise."[62]

Like all of the criticisms referenced here, the charge that liberal theology is "overly intellectual" has some merit. Liberal theology does often read and sound more like philosophy, and liberal theologians engaging sociopolitical questions on their own terms often fail to "say something theological."[63] And yet, this charge also deserves a rebuttal. The argument that liberal theology is overly intellectual is most often linked with corresponding descriptions of a faith that has no heart, that has "lost the experience of a personal God," [64] and is one of the underlying causes for the death of the staid mainline church. I recognize that thinking critically about faith may not be a stirring part of everyone's worship experience. Indeed, such critical thinking can be downright sobering. But there is also a deep and beautiful connection between reason and faith that such criticisms discount. Speaking personally, I have had countless experiences of encountering a new idea that stirs my heart, of coming to a new understanding that buoys my spirit. Sometimes these religious moments (and they are undoubtedly religious) occur while studying in solitude. Other times, they occur in a more philosophical conversation. And still other times, I experience this kind of spiritual uplift in the course of a very thoughtful and seemingly dispassionate sermon.

These moments arise most often in a process that includes deconstruction of some kind. I rarely experience a new thought or spiritual uplift like this without first having a preconception challenged. In other words, these truly religious moments do not happen because my faith is being affirmed start to finish. They happen because my understanding of the Scriptures, my sense of God's calling, and my set of spiritual practices are being challenged in some way. The absolutely essential feature of liberal theology—one that I defend without qualification—is that faith is always the starting point for a conversation, never the final word. This is the whole premise of theological education, in my view. Students arrive in our classroom with some kind of faith more or less intact, and we greet them by responding: OK, let's examine that faith. What Scriptures inform it and what informs your interpretation of the Scriptures?

What historical traditions have shaped your community of faith? What life experiences or other commitments affect the way you put your faith into practice?

This does not mean that all aspects of faith can and should conform to human reason. I believe that God's peace and love surpass human understanding. But it does mean that critical investigation of one's faith is a form of discipleship, not an obstacle to it. Now, one requirement to practicing this form of discipleship is a sense of humility that liberal theology has not always embodied. Indeed, one can practice critical inquiry with a prideful disposition that distinguishes between rational and irrational ideas and concepts, and discounts all aspects of human experience that fall into the latter camp. The charge that liberal theology is overly intellectual, I think, arises from the perception that this more prideful form is its only expression. I hope that this chapter offers a way to abide by the liberal call to critical inquiry, yet temper it with humility such that one sincerely practices "faith seeking understanding."[65]

Faith That Transforms Politics

In the months leading up to the 2004 election, the Reverend Dr. James Forbes of Riverside Church in New York City and Mobilization 2004 called for progressive Christians to speak more openly about their faith with their secular liberal counterparts, and he interpreted reluctance to do so as embarrassment.[1] His speech sparked a process of self-examination, which resulted in the idea for this book. In myself, I recognized the reluctance that Dr. Forbes named, but I did not agree that embarrassment was its cause. Instead, I identified theological and ethical commitments that complicate faith-explicit activism. As I worked to understand these commitments, I discovered how deeply I believed in their inherent value and in their transformative potential. Therefore, I try to respond to Dr. Forbes's invitation and to remain faithful to the three commitments identified in this book: to bring faith into the public square in a way that embodies a love that risks not being reciprocated, that acknowledges moral ambiguity and seeks shared concerns, and that practices theological humility by being honest, transparent, and accountable.

While the genesis and most particular context of the book is the increase of progressive Christian political activism, the questions addressed here stretch far beyond this particular time and circumstance. Indeed, they are perennial questions about the relationship between faith and politics. How should people of faith bring their religious convictions to bear on political questions? To what extent should religious sources remain authoritative as one moves into secular contexts? Should religious influences on our public positions be made plain and also subject to the process of critical inquiry and open debate? If we understand faith to be one of many informing and authoritative sources, then how do we negotiate between these sources when they are in disagreement? Is it appropriate for faith to trump the other sources of knowledge in matters of public policy? How do we seek consonance between the ideals and teachings of Scripture and contemporary public policy decisions, given the chasm between the contexts of Scripture and our own time and place?

These questions are both complicated and complicating. Therefore, when we are trying to gain political momentum, we often shove them aside as "academic" (meaning not pertaining to the real world), as hindrances and justification for inaction, and ultimately as politically disempowering. After listening to me present the material in this book at a conference, a woman in the audience responded with impatience and frustration. She said, "I work on Capitol Hill, and we [the religious left] are getting killed up there." People of faith are trying to make a real difference in a system that does not respond to love, ambiguity, and humility. Trying to work in this system and abide by these commitments is like entering a swim meet with leg weights. The easy response to this woman and those she represents is to say that mine is a call to faithful discipleship, not to political effectiveness.

I do believe this, but I also think that making this point as a response to this woman's criticism is not entirely fair. Those working for change on Capitol Hill (and in every state assembly and city hall) are trying to live out their commitments to faithful discipleship by advocating for public policies that truly enact love for the poor, care for the marginalized, and sanctuary for the sojourner. Changing those policies and electing the people who will maintain them are indeed acts of discipleship, but they are not the whole of it.

Discipleship also requires attention to the narrative that is larger than a legislative cycle, to the forms of human caring that are not captured in policy debates, and to the many contexts of human interaction that are not regulated by talking points and *Robert's Rules of Order*. In other words, discipleship reminds us that the behaviors that politics deems necessary may be effective relative to that particular context, but they are not therefore rendered good in an absolute sense. Antagonistic debate, clear and unequivocal statements, and divine endorsement may be effective given the structures of politics. (After all, it is what the opponent is doing.) However, if we grant effectiveness the highest value and stop questioning the goodness of these practices, then we also accept the context that mandates them. We foreclose the opportunity of transformation. By directing our attention to the larger narratives, discipleship reminds us that these behaviors are relative to a particular context and not inherently good, and that the context itself should be part of an ongoing process of transformation. Discipleship thus liberates us from the horror of the fixed[2] and requires us to act accordingly.

The questions and commitments that fill this book do not preclude political activism. They complicate it, and they may slow us down and dampen our fiery rhetoric. But the fear that we cannot act and practice critical reflection at the same time is unwarranted.

For example, I am constantly reflecting on how to be a good parent, but I do not stop caring for my children while I wrestle with these questions. Why then would we assume that we cannot continue to act for social justice, even while we reflect critically on the questions posed earlier? We can do both; indeed, we must. Questions like these are not preliminary concerns to politically engaged faith, but rather the very stuff of it. These questions—and others that the three commitments precipitate—are constant companions to faithful political engagement, not matters to be settled at the outset and then shelved once the real work begins.

Embodying these commitments *as we act* changes our political behavior in positive ways. Such reflection makes us more self-critical and open to dialogue with those who think and feel differently. Ongoing reflection that accompanies our action is likely to lessen our ability and desire to speak in absolute, dogmatic, or homogenous ways about "*the* Christian position." Wrestling with these and similar questions will heighten our awareness of and openness about the presence of moral ambiguity surrounding even our more certain positions. Honesty about the limitations of our knowledge and the processes of interpretation that are a part of faithful living will increase the humility with which we articulate religious convictions and their relationship to political questions.

Embodying these commitments can transform the contexts in which we act. I have confidence in the transformative potential of love, moral ambiguity, and theological humility because each one has the power to disrupt a pattern. Unconditional love disrupts a pattern of antagonism and division by insisting upon relationship and seeking the Christ in every person. When we determine to renounce hatred and to care for the well-being of all, we behave differently and we speak differently. We change the way in which we engage the opponent and the way we talk about the opponent when we are with like minds. Embodying unconditional love in sites of heated conflict changes the dynamic of the situation and contributes to a process of transformation.

Moral ambiguity also disrupts patterns of division by making us aware of shared concerns residing in the gray areas of our different positions. It also disrupts patterns of self-righteous insensitivity by holding us accountable to the mournful element in each decision and to the pain that our positions cause another person. Attention to moral ambiguity changes the dynamics from debate to conversation. And it changes the purpose of engaging different views from that of conversion to that of mutual understanding. And even in contexts where conversion or advocacy remains the purpose, attention to moral ambiguity reveals shared concerns that might issue in common ground and make reconciliation possible.

Theological humility disrupts the pattern of divine endorsement by reminding us that God's will reaches beyond our particular concern and partial conception. God's will may certainly include our own, but cannot be reduced to it. And so we make our theo-political claims with a sense of humility, aware of the limitations of perspective, transparent about our processes of interpretation, and accountable to other sources of knowledge. This changes the dynamic so that faith enters the public square as a participant, with all of the rights and responsibilities that entails. This behavior disrupts patterns of religious authoritarianism and makes the nonviolent presence of religion in the public square possible.

My hope for transformation is not only sustained by confidence in the power of these three commitments, but it is also rooted in belief that the world we know is ever-changing. We do not live out our lives in paradox, under conditions that are fixed and thus require compromise. Rather, I believe that our lives—and the structures that shape them—are in process, and that our actions affect the way in which process unfolds. This is the larger narrative that I alluded to earlier. The criticism that these less politically effective behaviors are somehow irresponsible *given our present situation* neglects the larger narrative and locks in place the current circumstances. Once we begin to see the future as unfolding rather than fixed, then we see our most immediate action as helping to determine the course. When I repeat the antagonistic, dogmatic, or authoritarian act because it is what this immediate situation requires, then I ensure that the next moment presents the self-same dilemma. If I act, however, in a different way, I open up a possibility for change. Like learning, the possibility of transformation requires the interruption of habituated thinking[3] and doing.

In closing, I offer an artistic image of such interruption, one that literally transformed sculpture by setting it in motion. In 1932, the sculptor Alexander Calder spoke at the opening of an exhibit that announced him as the inventor of a new art form, the mobile. He asked, "Why must art be static? You look at an abstraction, sculptured or painted. . . . It would be perfect but it is always still. The next step is sculpture in motion."[4] Even if you are unfamiliar with Calder's name, you have likely seen one of his large, red or black, metal and wire installations moving in gentle ways above your head in an atrium somewhere. The French word *mobile* carries a double meaning that Calder liked: as an adjective, it means movable; as a noun, it means motive. The mobile is both movable and something that spurs action. It is a structure designed to move and to motivate. Calder described his design process this way: "When I cut out my [metal] plates, I have two things in mind. I want them to be more alive, and I think about balance. . . . The most important thing is that the mobile be able to catch the air. It has to be able to move."[5] Faith, too, must catch the air so that it can interrupt the habits of hatred, over-simplification, and theological bravado that pervade our religious-political conversations. As long as we con-form our faith to the poblematic features of politics, it simply main-tains a shape rather than motivating something new. The image for faith in politics must be one informed by mobiles rather than still sculpture, by structures designed to catch the air, interrupt habits, and move in new ways.

N OTES

Introduction

1. This language is used regularly at my church, All Saints Episcopal Church in Pasadena, California.
2. Glen Stassen and David Gushee emphasize this point in their discussion of "salt, light, and deeds." Glen J. Stassen and David P. Gushee, *Kingdom Ethics: Following Jesus in Contemporary Context* (Downers Grove, Ill.: InterVarsity Press, 2003), 467–83.

1. Love

1. Anders Nygren, *Agape and Eros* (London: SPCK House, 1932, 1938, 1939; Philadelphia: Westminster Press, 1953). For a helpful overview and critical analysis, see William Werpehowski, "Anders Nygren's *Agape and Eros*," *The Oxford Handbook of Theological Ethics*, eds. Gilbert Meilaender and William Werpehowski. (Oxford: Oxford University Press, 2005), 443–48.
2. Reinhold Niebuhr, *An Interpretation of Christian Ethics* (San Francisco: Harper and Bros., 1935, 1963).
3. Gene Outka, *Agape: An Ethics Analysis* (New Haven, Conn.: Yale University Press, 1972). See also Gene Outka, "Universal Love and Impartiality," *The Love Commandments: Essays in Christian Ethics and Moral Philosophy*, eds. Edmund N. Santurri and William Werpehowski (Washington: Georgetown University Press, 1992), 1–103.
4. Margaret Farley, "New Patterns of Relationship: Beginnings of a Moral Revolution," *Woman: New Dimensions*, ed. Walter Burkhardt (New York: Paulist Press, 1975). Farley continues this critical and constructive work even into her most recent book, *Just Love: A Framework for Christian Sexual Ethics* (New York: Continuum, 2006).
5. Outka, "Universal Love," 8.
6. Judith Buter, *Precarious Life: The Powers of Mourning and Violence* (London: Verso, 2004, 2006), 89–90.
7. Mahatma Gandhi, *The Essential Gandhi: An Anthology of His Writings on His Life, Work and Ideas*, Vintge Books edition, ed. Louis Fischer (New York: Vintage Books, 1962), 199.
8. Rex Ambler, "Gandhian Peacemaking," *A Reader in Peace Studies*, eds. Paul Smoker, Ruth Davies, Barbara Munske (Oxford: Pergamon Press, 1990), 201 (my italics).
9. Martin Luther King, Jr., *Stride toward Freedom: The Montgomery Story* (New York: Harper and Bros., 1958), 104.
10. Ibid., 87.
11. Joan V. Bondurant, *Conquest of Violence: The Gandhian Philosophy of Conflict*, new revised edition (Princeton: Princeton University Press, 1958; 1988), 24.

12. Gandhi, *Essential*, 207.
13. Thich Nhat Hanh, *Being Peace* (Berkeley: Parallax Press, 1987; 1996), 86–87.
14. Ibid., 45.
15. Desmond Mpilo Tutu, *No Future without Forgiveness* (New York: Doubleday, 1999), 31.
16. King, *Stride*, 84–85 (my italics).
17. Ibid., 103.
18. Ibid., 104–5.
19. Ibid., 105.
20. Ibid., 106.
21. Ibid., 96–97.
22. Gandhi, *Essential*, 87.
23. Quoted in Joan V. Bondurant, *Conquest of Violence: The Gandhian Philosophy of Conflict*, revised edition (Princeton: Princeton University Press, 1988), 39.
24. Mohandas K. Gandhi, "On Nonviolence," *Peace and War*, ed. Charles R. Beitz and Theodore Herman (San Francisco: W. H. Freeman and Co., 1973), 246.
25. Gandhi, *Essential*, 207.
26. Bondurant, *Conquest of Violence*, 23.
27. Ibid., 24.
28. Ibid., 25–26.
29. Martin Luther King, Jr., *Why We Can't Wait* (New York: Mentor, 1963), 64.
30. Bondurant, *Conquest of Violence*, 39.
31. King, *Stride*, 102.
32. Ibid.
33. Ibid., 103 (my italics).
34. Quoted in Rosetta Ross, *Witnessing and Testifying* (Minneapolis: Fortress Press, 2003), 188.
35. King, *Stride*, 106.
36. Thich Nhat Hanh, *Being Peace*, 85.
37. Thich Nhat Hanh, *Interbeing: Fourteen Guidelines for Engaged Buddhism*, 3rd edition, ed. Fred Eppsteiner (Berkeley: Parallax Press, 1998), ix.
38. Hanh, *Being Peace*, 89–103.
39. Hanh, *Interbeing*, 3.
40. Ibid., 4.
41. Ibid., 5.
42. Ibid., 6.
43. Hanh, *Being Peace*, 86–87.
44. Tutu, *No Future*, 31.
45. Kasonga wa Kasonga, "The Meaning and Scope of *Ubuntu*," *Worlds of Memory and Wisdom: Encounters of Jews and African Christians*, eds. Jean Halpérin and Hans Ucko (Geneva: World Council of Church Publications, 2005), 125.
46. Kasonga, "Meaning," 126.
47. Ibid.
48. Tutu, *No Future*, 31.
49. Michael Battle, *Reconciliation: The Ubuntu Theology of Desmond Tutu* (Cleveland: Pilgrim Press, 1997), 5.

50. Ibid., 44.
51. Tutu, *No Future*, 31.
52. Hanh, *Being Peace*, 89.
53. Debbie Roberts, "Chapter Six: Lessons from the South African Truth and Reconciliation Commission," *Toward a Feminist Vision: A Critical Appraisal of Conflict Resolution Theory and Methodology* (doctoral dissertation, Claremont Graduate University, 2007).
54. John W. De Gruchy, *Reconciliation: Restoring Justice* (Minneapolis: Fortress Press, 2002), 28.
55. Catholic Worker, "The Aims and Means of the Catholic Worker Movement," *The Catholic Worker* (May 1990): 5.
56. Borden Parker Bowne, *Personalism* (New York: Houghton, Mifflin, & Co., 1908).
57. Joseph Amato, *Mounier and Maritain: A French Catholic Understanding of the Modern World*, Studies in the Humanities No. 6 Philosophy (Tuscaloosa: University of Alabama Press, 1975), 1.
58. Dorothy Day, *The Long Loneliness: The Autobiography of Dorothy Day*, reprint of the 1952 edition (San Francisco: Harper & Row, 1981), 171.
59. Mel Piehl, *Breaking Bread: The Catholic Worker and the Origin of Catholic Radicalism in America* (Philadelphia: Temple University Press, 1982), 97.
60. Patrick Coy, "The One-Person Revolution of Ammon Hennacy," *A Revolution of the Heart: Essays on the Catholic Worker*, ed. Patrick G. Coy (Philadelphia: Temple University Press, 1988), 159.
61. Day, *Long Loneliness*, 171.
62. Daniel C. Maguire, *A Moral Creed for All Christians* (Minneapolis: Fortress Press, 2005), 197.
63. Walter Wink, *Violence and Nonviolence in South Africa: Jesus' Third Way* (Philadelphia: New Society Publishers, 1987).
64. Thich Nhat Hanh, "Ahimsa: The Path of Harmlessness," *Buddhist Peacework: Creating Cultures of Peace*, ed. David W. Chappell (Boston: Wisdom Publications, 1999), 155.
65. James M. Gustafson, *Theology and Christian Ethics* (Philadelphia: United Church Press, 1974), 132.
66. Day, *Long Loneliness*, 171.
67. Hanh, *Being Peace*, 14–15.
68. Ellen Ott Marshall, "Practicing Imagination," *Choosing Peace through Daily Practices* (Cleveland: Pilgrim Press, 2005), 65–85.
69. Bondurant, *Conquest of Violence*, 40.
70. King, *Why*, 78.
71. Ibid., 63.
72. Gandhi, *Essential*, 168.
73. Ibid., 192–93.
74. Bob Edgar, *Middle Church: Reclaiming the Moral Values of the Faithful Majority from the Religious Right* (New York: Simon and Schuster Paperbacks, 2006).
75. Bill Moyers, "A Time for Heresy," speech delivered at Divinity School of Wake Forest, Winston-Salem, North Carolina (March 14, 2006), http://divinity.wfu.edu/transcript_20060314a.html.

76. This is a persistent theme in the sermons of Rector Ed Bacon of All Saints Church in Pasadena. I am indebted to him for clarifying the importance of this broader theological context and embodying the difference it makes in one's work for peace and justice.

2. Moral Ambiguity

1. James M. Gustafson, *Ethics from a Theocentric Perspective*, Vol. 2, *Ethics and Theology* (Chicago: University of Chicago Press, 1984), 19.
2. Ibid.
3. The Associated Press, "In the Pilot's Words: 'Villages Set on Fire,'" *New York Times* (April 16, 1999): A9.
4. Michael R. Gordon, "NATO Admits the Mistaken Bombing of Civilians," *New York Times* (April 16, 1999): A1, A9.
5. National Conference of Catholic Bishops, *The Challenge of Peace: God's Promise and Our Response: A Pastoral Letter on War and Peace* (Washington: United States Catholic Conference, July 8, 1983; sixth printing, Washington: United States Catholic Conference, January 20, 1984), 31.
6. Aristotle, *Nicomachean Ethics*, trans. Martin Ostwald (Englewood Cliffs, N.J.: Prentice Hall, 1962), 3.1.
7. Michael Walzer, *Just and Unjust Wars: A Moral Argument with Historical Illustrations*, 3rd edition (New York: Basic Books, 1977), 153.
8. Aristotle, *Nicomachean Ethics*, 3.1.1110b.20.
9. Goran Tomasevic (photographer with Reuters) *New York Times* (April 15, 1999): A13.
10. Unnamed photographer, *New York Times* (April 15, 1999): A13.
11. Anja Niedringhaus (photographer with Agence France-Presse) *New York Times* (April 16, 1999): A1.
12. Martha C. Nussbaum, *Love's Knowledge: Essays on Philosophy and Literature* (New York: Oxford University Press, 1990), 40.
13. Ibid., referencing Aristotle.
14. Alison M. Jaggar. "Love and Knowledge: Emotion in Feminist Epistemology," *Women, Knowledge and Reality: Explorations in Feminist Philosophy*, eds. Ann Garry and Marilyn Pearsall (Boston: Unwin Hyman, 1989), 139.
15. Ibid., 137.
16. Nussbaum, *Love's Knowledge*, 291.
17. Ibid.
18. Ibid., 42.
19. Margaret A. Farley, "The Role of Experience in Moral Discernment," *Christian Ethics: Problems and Prospects*, eds. Lisa Sowle Cahill and James F. Childress (Cleveland: Pilgrim Press, 1996), 134.
20. James Gustafson, "The Place of Scripture in Christian Ethics: A Methodological Study," *Theology and Christian Ethics* (Philadelphia: Pilgrim Press, 1974), 121–46.

21. Douglas F. Ottati, *Jesus Christ and Christian Vision* (Minneapolis: Fortress Press, 1989), 34.
22. Gustafson, "The Place of Scripture," 133.
23. Ibid., 134.
24. Ibid., 134–35.
25. Stanley Hauerwas, *A Community of Character: Toward a Constructive Christian Social Ethic* (South Bend, Ind.: University of Notre Dame, 1981).
26. Jeffrey Stout. "Tradition in Ethics," *Westminster Dictionary of Christian Ethics*, eds. James F. Childress and John Macquarrie (Louisville: Westminster John Knox Press, 1986), 62.
27. Ottati, *Jesus Christ and Christian Vision*, 5. For more on tradition, see Philip Turner, "Tradition in the Church," *The Oxford Handbook of Theological Ethics*, eds. Gilbert Meilaender and William Werpehowski (Oxford: Oxford University Press, 2005), 130–47; David Hollenbach, S.J., "Tradition, Historicity, and Truth in Theological Ethics," *Christian Ethics: Problems and Prospects*, eds. Lisa Sowle Cahill and James F. Childress (Cleveland: The Pilgrim Press, 1996), 60–75.
28. James Gustafson, "The Relationship of Empirical Science to Moral Thought," *From Christ to the World: Introductory Readings in Christian Ethics*, eds. Wayne G. Boulton, Thomas D. Kennedy, and Allen Verhey (Grand Rapids, Mich.: Eerdmans, 1994), 165.
29. Ibid., 166.
30. Ibid., 167.
31. Ibid., 168.
32. Farley, "Role," 135.
33. Ibid., 136.
34. Ibid.
35. Nussbaum, *Love's Knowledge*, 42.
36. Farley, "Role," 146.
37. Ibid.
38. Bernard Arthur Owen Williams, *Problems of the Self: Philosophical Papers (1956–1972)* (Cambridge: Cambridge University Press), 1973. I am grateful to Rustin Comer for bringing this material to my attention.
39. Carol Gilligan, "Moral Orientation and Moral Development," *Justice and Care: Essential Readings in Feminist Ethics*, ed. Virginia Held (Boulder, Colo.: Westview Press, 1995).
40. These questions reflect what Margaret Urban Walker refers to in *Moral Contexts* (Lanham, Md.: Rowman & Littlefied, 2003) as the alternative epistemology of feminist ethics, which is characterized by three features: "attention to the particular; a way of constructing morally relevant understandings which is 'contextual and narrative'; a picture of deliberation as a site of expression and communication" (72).
41. James M. Gustafson, *Ethics from a Theocentric Perspective*, Vol. 2, *Ethics and Theology* (Chicago: University of Chicago Press, 1984), 21.
42. Walter Wink, *The Powers That Be: Theology for a New Millennium* (New York: Doubleday, 1998; New York: Galilee, 1999), 165.

43. Phillip J. Wogaman, *Christian Perspectives on Politics* (Louisville: Westminster John Knox Press, 2000), 138.

44. Bob Edgar, *Middle Church: Reclaiming the Moral Values of the Faithful Majority from the Religious Right* (New York: Simon and Schuster Paperbacks, 2006), 231.

45. Edgar, *Middle Church*, 10. Jim Wallis clarifies his position on page 11 of *God's Politics* and devotes parts three and four of the book to war and poverty. See Jim Wallis, *God's Politics: Why the Right Gets It Wrong and the Left Doesn't Get It: A New Vision for Faith and Politics in America* (San Francisco: Harper San Francisco, 2005).

46. Helen Prejean, *Dead Man Walking: An Eyewitness Account of the Death Penalty in the United States*, first Vintage Books edition (New York: Vintage Books, 1994), xi.

47. Michael B. Katz, *The Undeserving Poor: From the War on Poverty to the War on Welfare* (New York: Pantheon Books, 1989), 9.

48. Mary Elizabeth Hobgood, *Dismantling Privilege: An Ethics of Accountability* (Cleveland: Pilgrim Press, 2000), 6.

49. Ibid., 10.

50. James Gustafson, *Ethics from a Theocentric Perspective*. Vol. 1, *Ethics and Theology* (Chicago: University of Chicago Press, 1981), 268.

51. Sallie McFague, *Life Abundant: Rethinking Theology and Economy for a Planet in Peril* (Minneapolis: Fortress Press, 2001), 154.

52. John B. Cobb, Jr., "Ensuring Sustainability," *Justice in a Global Economy: Strategies for Home, Community, and World*, eds. Pamela K. Brubaker, Rebecca Todd Peters, and Laura A. Stivers (Louisville: Westminster John Knox Press, 2006), 141.

53. Prejean, *Dead Man Walking*, 13.

54. Ibid., 28.

55. Ibid., 21.

56. Ibid., 31.

57. See, for example, Roger Fisher and William Ury, *Getting to Yes: Negotiating Agreement without Giving In*, second edition, ed. Bruce Patton (New York: Penguin Books, 1991), 40–55.

58. Prejean, *Dead Man Walking*, 20–21.

59. Carol Lakey Hess, "Between Advocacy and Dialogue: Peacebuilding in the Classroom," *Choosing Peace through Daily Practices*, ed. Ellen Ott Marshall (Cleveland: Pilgrim Press, 2005), 106–28. Hess also discusses this in "Echo's Lament: Teaching, Mentoring, and the Dangers of Narcissistic Pedagogy," *Teaching Theology & Religion* 6, no. 3 (July 2003): 127–37.

3. Theological Humility

1. Jim Wallis, *God's Politics: Why the Right Gets It Wrong and the Left Doesn't Get It* (San Francisco: HarperSanFrancisco, 2005).

2. See Ellen Ott Marshall, *Though the Fig Tree Does Not Blossom: Toward a Responsible Theology of Christian Hope* (Nashville: Abingdon Press, 2006).

3. George Stroup, "Revelation," *Christian Theology: An Introduction to Its Traditions and Tasks*, eds. Peter C. Hodgson and Robert H. King (Minneapolis: Fortress Press, 1994), 123.
4. Ibid., 114.
5. H. Richard Niebuhr, *The Meaning of Revelation* (New York: Macmillan Publishing Co., 1941), 78.
6. Ibid., 69.
7. Ibid., 71.
8. Ibid., 79.
9. Ibid., 70.
10. Ibid., 80.
11. Ibid.
12. Ibid., 16.
13. Ibid., 81, 83, 84.
14. Ibid., 5.
15. Ibid., 7.
16. Ibid., 13.
17. H. Richard Niebuhr, "Reflections on the Christian Theory of History," *Theology, History and Culture*. ed. William Stacy Johnson (New Haven: Yale University Press, 1996), 82–83.
18. Gary Dorrien, *The Making of American Liberal Theology: Idealism, Realism, and Modernity, 1900–1950* (Louisville: Westminster John Knox Press, 2003), 1.
19. Dorothee Soelle, *Thinking about God* (London: SCM Press, 1990), 14.
20. Ernst Troeltsch, "Historical and Dogmatic Method," *Religion in History*, trans. James Luther Adams and Walter F. Bense (Minneapolis: Fortress Press, 1991), 16.
21. Konrad Hecker, "Liberalism and Liberal Theology," *Encyclopedia of Theology: The Concise* Sacramentum Mundi, ed. Karl Rahner (New York: The Seabury Press, 1975), 842.
22. Wallis, *God's Politics*, 212.
23. According to historical theologian Claude Welch, Ritschl was "the 'characteristic' man of the period, the embodiment of the late nineteenth century's effort to hold together personal faith, scientific history, and ethical demand and so present a view of Christianity intelligible and persuasive to modern culture." Claude Welch, *Protestant Thought in the Nineteenth Century*. Vol. 2, 1970–1914 (New Haven: Yale University Press, 1985), 2.
24. Welch, Vol. 2, 3.
25. Adolf von Harnack, *What Is Christianity?* (Philadelphia: Fortress Press, 1957), 298.
26. Ibid., 13–14.
27. Ibid., 14.
28. Ibid., 98–101.
29. Ernst Troeltsch, "What Does 'Essence of Christianity' Mean?" *Ernst Troeltsch: Writings on Theology and Religion*, trans. Michael Pye (Louisville: Westminster John Knox Press, 1977), 124.
30. Ibid., 128.
31. Ibid., 133.

32. Ibid., 166.

33. David Heim, "Voters and Values: The Divided Mind of the Religious Left," *Christian Century* 123, no.16 (2006): 27. Heim writes, "The religious left wants, at least at times, to offer a set of Christian values that parallels the right's but differs in content. But another element within the religious left is deeply uneasy about bringing religion directly into the political sphere."

34. Rosemary Radford Ruether, "Feminist Interpretation: A Method of Correlation," *Feminist Interpretation of the Bible*, ed. Letty M. Russell (Philadelphia: Westminster Press, 1985), 111.

35. James Gustafson, *Theology and Christian Ethics* (Philadelphia: United Church Press, 1974), 137.

36. Margaret Farley, "Feminist Consciousness and the Interpretation of Scripture," *Feminist Interpretation of the Bible*. ed. Letty M. Russell (Philadelphia: Westminster Press, 1985), 43.

37. Ibid.

38. Ibid., 44–45.

39. Traci C. West, *Disruptive Christian Ethics: When Racism and Women's Lives Matter* (Louisville: Westminster John Knox Press, 2006), 81.

40. Ibid., 82.

41. Ibid., 82–83.

42. Ibid., 82.

43. Glen Stassen and David Gushee, *Kingdom Ethics: Following Jesus in Contemporary Context* (Downers Grove, Ill.: InterVarsity Press, 2003), 92–93.

44. Ibid., 85.

45. Ibid.

46. Ibid., 89.

47. Ibid., 97.

48. Franklin I. Gamwell, *Politics as a Christian Vocation: Faith and Democracy Today* (Cambridge: Cambridge University Press, 2004).

49. Ibid., 4.

50. Ibid.

51. Ibid., 59.

52. Ibid., 44.

53. Thomas W. Ogletree, *The World Calling* (Louisville: Westminster John Knox Press, 2004), 39.

54. Elizabeth M. Bounds, *Coming Together/Coming Apart: Religion, Community, and Modernity* (New York: Routledge, 1997), 13.

55. Delwin Brown, "Introduction: What Progressive Christianity Is Not!" *Progressive Christian Beliefs: An Introduction for Liberals who are Searching, Conservatives who are Open, and Others who are Curious*, 2, http://progressivetheology.worldpress.com (accessed June 3, 2008).

56. Ibid., 2

57. Ibid., 13.

58. H. Richard Niebuhr, *Christ and Culture* (New York: Harper Torchbooks, 1951), 91.

59. John B. Cobb, Jr., "A Normative View of Progressive Christianity" (Berkeley: The Progressive Christian Witness, 2006), 5, http://www.progressivechristianwitness.org/pcw.cfm?id=37&p=5 (accessed March 19, 2007).

60. Ibid., 1. Cobb does identify the problematic features of liberalism and the ways in which progressive Christianity tries to move beyond them (7).

61. Dorrien, *The Making of American Liberal Theology*, 2.

62. Ibid., 8.

63. Stanley Hauerwas, "On Keeping Theological Ethics Theological," *From Christ to the World: Introductory Readings in Christian Ethics*, eds. Wayne G. Boulton, Thomas D. Kennedy, and Allen Verhey (Grand Rapids, Mich.: Eerdmans, 1994), 130.

64. Wallis, *God's Politics*, 34.

65. "Faith seeking understanding" as St. Anselm's definition of theology.

Conclusion

1. Juliana Finucane, "Religious Political Progressives Seek to Revive their Movement," *Religious News Service* (June 10, 2004), 2, http://www.american-progress.org (accessed August 20, 2004).

2. Annie Dillard, *Pilgrim at Tinker Creek*, first Perennial Classics Edition (New York: HarperCollins, 1974; New York: Perennial Classics, 1998), 66.

3. I am grateful to Dr. Daryl Smith for introducing me to this phrase from literature on cognitive complexity and learning.

4. Marla Prather, *Alexander Calder 1898–1976*, 2nd edition (Washington: National Gallery of Art; New Haven, Conn., and London: Yale University Press, 1998), 57.

5. Ibid., 231.

SELECTED BIBLIOGRAPHY

Amato, Joseph. *Mounier and Maritain: A French Catholic Understanding of the Modern World*. Studies in the Humanities No. 6 Philosophy. Tuscaloosa: The University of Alabama Press, 1975.

Ambler, Rex. "Gandhian Peacemaking," *A Reader in Peace Studies*, ed. Paul Smoker, Ruth Davies, Barbara Munske. Oxford: Pergamon Press, 1990.

Andolsen, Barbara Hilkert. "Agape in Feminist Ethics," *Feminist Theological Ethics: A Reader*, ed. Lois K. Daly. Louisville: Westminster John Knox Press, 1994.

Aristotle. *Nicomachean Ethics*,trans. Martin Ostwald. Englewood Cliffs: Prentice Hall, 1962.

Battle, Michael. *Reconciliation: The Ubuntu Theology of Desmond Tutu*. Cleveland: Pilgrim Press, 1997.

Beinart, Peter. *The Good Fight: Why Liberals—and Only Liberals—Can Win the War on Terror and Make America Great Again*. New York: HarperCollins, 2006.

Bondurant, Joan V. *Conquest of Violence: The Gandhian Philosophy of Conflict*, rev. ed. Princeton: Princeton University Press, 1988.

Bounds, Elizabeth M. *Coming Together/Coming Apart: Religion, Community, and Modernity*. New York: Routledge, 1997.

Brock, Rita Nakashima. *Journeys by Heart: A Christology of Erotic Power*. New York: Crossroad, 1996.

Brueggemann, Walter. *Mandate to Difference: An Invitation to the Contemporary Church*. Louisville: Westminster John Knox Press, 2007.

Carter, Jimmy. *Our Endangered Values: America's Moral Crisis*. New York: Simon and Schuster Paperbacks, 2005.

Cobb, John B., Jr. "Ensuring Sustainability," *Justice in a Global Economy: Strategies for Home, Community, and World*, ed. Pamela K. Brubaker, Rebecca Todd Peters, Laura A. Stivers. Louisville: Westminster John Knox Press, 2006.

———, ed. *Progressive Christians Speak: A Different Voice on Faith and Politics*. Louisville: Westminster John Knox Press, 2003. (Originally published 2000 under name *Speaking of Religion and Politics: The Progressive Church on Hot Topics* by Pinch Publications.)

Coy, Patrick. "The One-Person Revolution of Ammon Hennacy," *A Revolution of the Heart: Essays on the Catholic Worker*, ed. Patrick G. Coy. Philadelphia: Temple University Press, 1988.

———. Paper delivered at Women and Peace Conference at Juniata, 1999.

Day, Dorothy. *The Long Loneliness: The Autobiography of Dorothy Day*. 1952. Reprint. San Francisco: Harper & Row, 1981.

De Gruchy, John W. *Reconciliation: Restoring Justice*. Minneapolis: Fortress Press, 2002.

Dorrien, Gary. *The Making of American Liberal Theology: Idealism, Realism, and Modernity, 1900–1950*. Louisville: Westminster John Knox Press, 2003.

Edgar, Bob. *Middle Church: Reclaiming the Moral Values of the Faithful Majority from the Religious Right*. New York: Simon and Schuster Paperbacks, 2006.

Farley, Margaret A. *Compassionate Respect: A Feminist Approach to Medical Ethics and Other Questions*. New York: Paulist Press, 2002.

———. *Just Love: A Framework for Christian Sexual Ethics.* New York, Continuum, 2006.

———. "The Role of Experience in Moral Discernment," *Christian Ethics: Problems and Prospects*, ed. Lisa Sowle Chill and James F. Childress. Cleveland: The Pilgrim Press, 1996.

Gamwell, Franklin I. *Politics as a Christian Vocation: Faith and Democracy Today.* Cambridge: Cambridge University Press, 2005.

Gandhi, Mahatma. *The Essential Gandhi: An Anthology of his writings on his life, work and ideas*, Vintage Books Edition, ed. Louis Fischer. New York: Vintage Books, 1962.

Gandhi, Mohandas K., "On Nonviolence," *Peace and War*, ed. Charles R. Beitz and Theodore Herman. San Francisco: W. H. Freeman and Co., 1973.

———. *Satyagraha: Non-violent Resistance*, ed. Bharatan Kumarappa. New York: Schocken Books, 1961.

Gustafson, James M. *Ethics from a Theocentric Perspective*, Vol. 2: Ethics and Theology. Chicago: The University of Chicago Press, 1984.

———. *An Examined Faith: The Grace of Self-Doubt.* Minneapolis: Fortress Press, 2004.

———. *Theology and Christian Ethics.* Philadelphia: Pilgrim Press, 1974

Hanh, Thich Nhat. "Ahimsa: The Path of Harmlessness," *Buddhist Peacework: Creating Cultures of Peace*, ed. David W. Chappell. Boston: Wisdom Publications, 1999.

———. *Being Peace.* 1987. Berkeley: Parallax Press, 1996.

———. *Interbeing: Fourteen Guidelines for Engaged Buddhism*, 3rd ed. ed. Fred Eppsteiner. Berkeley: Parallax Press, 1987, 1998.

Harnack, Adolf von. *What is Christianity?* Philadelphia: Fortress Press, 1957.

Hecker, Konrad. "Liberalism and Liberal Theology," *Encyclopedia of Theology: The Concise Sacramentum Mundi.* ed., Karl Rahner. New York: The Seabury Press, 1975.

Hobgood, Mary Elizabeth. *Dismantling Privilege: An Ethics of Accountability.* Cleveland: The Pilgrim Press, 2000.

Kasonga, Kasonga wa. "The Meaning and Scope of *Ubuntu*," *Worlds of Memory and Wisdom: Encounters of Jews and African Christians*, ed. Jean Halpérin and Hans Ucko. Geneva: World Council of Churches Publications, 2005.

King, Martin Luther, Jr. *Stride toward Freedom: The Montgomery Story.* New York: Harper and Bros., 1958.

———. *Why We Can't Wait.* New York: Mentor, 1963.

Lakoff, George. *Don't Think of an Elephant: Know Your Values and Frame the Debate.* White River Junction, Vermont: Chelsea Green Publishing, 2004.

Lakoff, George and the Rockridge Institute. *Thinking Points: Communicating Our American Values and Vision.* New York: Farrar, Straus and Giroux, 2006.

Maguire, Daniel C. *A Moral Creed for All Christians.* Minneapolis: Fortress Press, 2005.

Malina, Bruce J. *The Social Gospel of Jesus: The Kingdom of God in Mediterranean Perspective.* Minneapolis: Fortress Press, 2001.

Marshall, Ellen Ott, ed. *Choosing Peace through Daily Practices.* Cleveland: Pilgrim Press, 2005.

———. *Though the Fig Tree Does Not Blossom: Toward a Responsible Theology of Christian Hope.* Nashville: Abingdon Press, 2006.

McFague, Sallie. *Life Abundant: Rethinking Theology and Economy for a Planet in Peril.* Minneapolis: Fortress Press, 2001.

Moyers, Bill. "A Time for Heresy." Speech at Divinity School of Wake Forest. Winston-Salem, North Carolina University. 14 March 2006, available from http://divinity.wfu.edu/transcript_20060314a.html.

National Conference of Catholic Bishops. *The Challenge of Peace: God's Promise and Our Response. A Pastoral Letter on War and Peace*. Washington, D.C.: United States Catholic Conference, 1983.

Niebuhr, H. Richard. *Christ and Culture*. New York: Harper Torchbooks, 1951.

———. *The Meaning of Revelation*. New York: Macmillan Publishing Co., Inc., 1941.

Nygren, Anders. *Agape and Eros*, trans. Philip S. Watson. Philadelphia: The Westminster Press, 1953.

Ogletree, Thomas W. *The World Calling: The Church's Witness in Politics and Society*. Louisville: Westminster John Knox Press, 2004.

Ottati, Douglas F. *Jesus Christ and Christian Vision*. Minneapolis: Fortress Press, 1989.

Outka, Gene. *Agape: An Ethical Analysis*. New Haven: Yale University Press, 1972.

Piehl, Mel. *Breaking Bread: The Catholic Worker and the Origin of Catholic Radicalism in America*. Philadelphia: Temple University Press, 1982.

Roberts, Debbie. *Toward a Feminist Vision: A Critical Appraisal of Conflict Resolution Theory and Methodology*. Doctoral dissertation, Claremont Graduate University, 2007.

Ross, Rosetta E. *Witnessing and Testifying: Black Women, Religion, and Civil Rights*. Minneapolis: Fortress Press, 2003.

Santurri, Edmund N. and William Wepehowski, eds. *The Love Commandments: Essays in Christian Ethics and Moral Philosophy*. Washington, D.C.: Georgetown University Press, 1992.

Stassen, Glen J. and David P. Gushee. *Kingdom Ethics: Following Jesus in Contemporary Context*. Downers Grove: InterVarsity Press, 2003.

Stroup, George. "Revelation," *Christian Theology: An Introduction to Its Traditions and Tasks*, ed. Peter C. Hodgson and Robert H. King. Minneapolis: Fortress Press, 1994.

Troeltsch, Ernst. "Historical and Dogmatic Method in Theology," *Religion in History*, trans. James Luther Adams and Walter F. Bense. Minneapolis: Fortress Press, 1991.

———. "What Does 'Essence of Christianity' Mean?" *Ernst Troeltsch: Writings on Theology and Religion*, trans. Michael Pye. Louisville: Westminster John Knox Press, 1977.

Tutu, Desmond Mpilo. *No Future without Forgiveness*. New York: Doubleday, 1999.

Wallis, Jim. *God's Politics: Why the Right Gets It Wrong and the Left Doesn't Get It*. New York: HarperSanFrancisco, 2005.

Walzer, Michael. *Just and Unjust Wars: A Moral Argument with Historical Illustrations*, 3rd ed. New York: Basic Books, 1977.

Welch, Claude. *Protestant Thought in the Nineteenth Century*. Vol. 1, 1799–1870. New Haven: Yale University Press, 1972.

———. *Protestant Thought in the Nineteenth Century*. Vol. 2, 1970–1914. New Haven, Conn.: Yale University Press, 1985.

West, Traci C. *Disruptive Christian Ethics: When Racism and Women's Lives Matter*. Louisville: Westminster John Knox Press, 2006.

Wink, Walter. *The Powers That Be: Theology for a New Millennium*. New York: Doubleday, 1998; New York: Galilee, 1999.

———. *Violence and Nonviolence in South Africa: Jesus' Third Way*. Philadelphia: New Society Publishers, 1987.

Wogaman, J. Phillip. *Christian Perspectives on Politics*. Louisville: Westminster John Knox Press, 2000.

Zwick, Mark and Louise. *The Catholic Worker Movement: Intellectual and Spiritual Origins*. New York: Paulist Press, 2005.

Index